THE
AUBERGINE
COOKBOOK

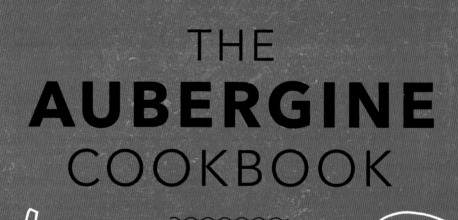

THE
AUBERGINE
COOKBOOK

HEATHER THOMAS

EBURY
PRESS

CONTENTS

SUPPERS

BAKING & PRESERVES

INTRODUCTION

Once known as the 'poor man's meat', the humble aubergine has been elevated to the status of a 'superfood' and is now a sought-after item on the menus of even the smartest restaurants. The popularity of the aubergine (or 'eggplant' as it's called in the United States; *brinjal* in India and southeast Asia; and *melanzane* in Italy) reflects the new lighter way of eating, with its focus on vegetables and plant protein. And the growing demand for healthy Mediterranean and Middle Eastern food has helped to propel the aubergine into the culinary mainstream in recent years.

VARIETIES

Technically, aubergines are not really vegetables at all, but are classed as 'fruits' from the nightshade family (*Solanaceae*). They are available in a variety of shapes and colours, ranging from the ubiquitous purple oval specimens that most of us see on supermarket shelves, to the small, rounded ivory-white ones from Asia that triggered their alternative name of 'eggplant'. Aubergines can be large, medium or small; oval, round, squat, bulbous or long and slender; white, greenish-white, green, yellowish, violet, purple or black.

ORIGINS & GEOGRAPHY

Due to its bulk and spongy texture, Sicilians call the aubergine 'the meat of the earth', and it's a staple of the healthy cuisine of the region that spans from Spain in the west, right round the shores of the Mediterranean Sea through southern France, Italy, Greece, the Levant and North Africa. However, the aubergine originated in Asia, where it grew wild, then was first cultivated in China in the fifth century BC. Its popularity later spread to the Middle East and it wasn't introduced into southern Europe until the early Middle Ages.

NUTRITION

A good source of dietary fibre and vitamins A, B6, B12, folic acid, C and K as well as minerals including calcium, copper, iron, manganese, magnesium and potassium, aubergines can make a valuable contribution to a healthy diet, especially as they are low in calories, virtually fat-free and help to lower cholesterol. They are rich in antioxidants, including nasunin, which not only gives the aubergine its purple hue but also helps to protect our brain cells, so that they function properly.

COOKING & PREPARATION

The aubergine is an extremely versatile vegetable; not only can it be roasted, grilled (broiled), baked, fried, pickled, stuffed and puréed, it can also be transformed into healthy 'fries', sliders, mini pizza bases or even 'fakon' (a smoked aubergine substitute for bacon, see page 27).

When the aubergine is cooked the spongy flesh softens and becomes silky and buttery in texture. It has a pleasant, mild flavour with a subtle hint of smokiness, which is enhanced by spices and herbs. Pre-salting the cut flesh tenderises it and helps to reduce its natural bitterness, while also preventing it soaking up too much oil during frying. However, as most of us lead busy lives and are always time-challenged – and modern varieties of aubergines tend to be less bitter – there is no need to pre-salt them unless specified in a recipe.

INTERNATIONAL CUISINE

Aubergines have long been the major ingredient in many classic Mediterranean dishes, including baba ganoush, imam bayildi, melanzane alla parmigiana, caponata, ratatouille and moussaka.

Here we have collected recipes from around the world to create this anthology, incorporating the latest trends as well as traditional dishes. There are pickles, chutneys and curries from India, where aubergine is added to dal and stews or roasted, mashed and flavoured with spices; spicy Szechuan and sweet and sour dishes from China; green coconut curries from Thailand; and sticky miso-glazed aubergine from Japan. From the Middle East, we have Turkish, Persian, Lebanese and Israeli classic dishes, augmented with pomegranate molasses, warming spices (sumac and za'atar) and yoghurt. The Maghreb countries contribute couscous dishes and roasted salads flavoured with ras el hanout. And, of course, we have the Spanish escalivada salad, ratatouille and tian from Provence, Italian aubergine bakes and pasta sauces, and moussaka and creamy melitzanosalata from Greece.

We even have an aubergine chocolate cake. This is the ultimate cookbook for everyone who loves aubergines and wants to eat them as part of a delicious, healthy diet.

SNACKS & STARTERS

AUBERGINE 'FRIES' WITH BALSAMIC GLAZE

SERVES: 4 | **PREP:** 10 MINUTES | **COOK:** 1 HOUR

2 large aubergines
(eggplants), trimmed
4 tbsp olive oil
sea salt, to season
balsamic glaze, for drizzling

These delicious, crispy aubergine 'fries' are oven-baked instead of deep-fried, so they are much healthier and less oily than traditional potato fries. They are quick and easy to prepare and make a great snack or accompaniment to pre-dinner drinks.

1 Preheat the oven to 200°C, 400°F, gas mark 6. Line 2 baking trays (cookie sheets) with baking parchment (parchment paper).

2 Cut the aubergines in half lengthways. Cut each half into long 'chips' about 1cm (½in) thick.

3 Spread the aubergine chips out on the lined baking trays, leaving some space in between them so they crisp up nicely. Drizzle the oil over the top, turning the chips in the oil to coat them lightly. Sprinkle with the salt.

4 Bake in the oven for about 1 hour, turning them once or twice, until they are crisp and golden brown.

5 Remove from the oven and drizzle the balsamic glaze over them. Serve hot or warm.

OR YOU CAN TRY THIS...
– Sprinkle with a flavoured salt, e.g. coriander, lemon or chilli salt.
– Sprinkle the chips with sesame seeds before baking.
– Scatter some finely chopped herbs over the chips, e.g. parsley, coriander or mint.
– Serve with seedy fennel or mint yoghurt, tzatziki, a creamy goat's cheese dip or hummus.
– Dust with paprika (sweet or smoked), ground cumin, cayenne or sumac and za'atar.
– Drizzle with a good-quality balsamic vinegar or even some honey.

AUBERGINE 'CRISPS' WITH FENNEL YOGHURT DIP

SERVES: 4 | **PREP:** 15 MINUTES | **COOK:** 1 HOUR

2 large aubergines
    (eggplants), trimmed
4 tbsp olive oil
2 tbsp pine nuts
sea salt and freshly ground
    black pepper

For the fennel yoghurt dip:
2 tsp fennel seeds
200g/7oz (scant 1 cup)
    0%-fat Greek yoghurt
1 garlic clove, crushed
2 tsp lemon juice
1 tbsp olive oil
a few sprigs of fennel herb,
    chopped

You can make these 'crisps' as thin or as chunky as you like – the thicker they are the longer they will take to cook and crisp up. If you're in a hurry, you can shallow-fry them in olive oil and then drain on kitchen paper (paper towels). However, they will absorb more oil.

1 Preheat the oven to 200°C, 400°F, gas mark 6. Line 2 baking trays (cookie sheets) with baking parchment (parchment paper).

2 Cut the aubergines into rounds – no more than 5mm (¼in) max (thinner if you want them really crisp).

3 Spread the aubergine slices out on the lined baking trays, leaving some space in between them so they crisp up nicely. Drizzle the oil over the top, turning the rounds in the oil to coat them lightly. Sprinkle with sea salt and grind some black pepper over.

4 Bake in the oven for about 1 hour, turning them once or twice, until they are really crisp and golden brown.

5 Meanwhile, make the fennel yoghurt dip: Heat a small frying pan over a medium heat and add the fennel seeds. Dry-fry for about 2 minutes, tossing gently, until they release their aroma. Remove from the pan immediately and crush them in a pestle and mortar. Mix with the remaining ingredients, then cover and chill in the fridge.

6 Add the pine nuts to a dry frying pan and dry-fry for 1–2 minutes, tossing occasionally, until golden brown and aromatic. Take care not to let them burn. Remove from the pan and set aside to cool.

7 Serve the aubergine 'crisps' warm or cold with the fennel yoghurt dip and sprinkled with the toasted pine nuts.

OR YOU CAN TRY THIS...
– Squeeze a little lemon juice over the 'crisps' just before serving.

AUBERGINE FRITTERS WITH HONEY

SERVES: 4 | **PREP:** 15 MINUTES | **SALT:** 30 MINUTES | **COOK:** 15 MINUTES

2 large aubergines
    (eggplants)
sea salt, for sprinkling
olive oil, for shallow-frying
clear Greek honey,
    for drizzling
lemon wedges, to serve

For the batter:
125g/4oz (1¼ cups) plain
    (all-purpose) flour
1 tsp baking powder
1 medium free-range egg
1 tbsp olive oil
150ml/5floz (generous
    ½ cup) water
a pinch of dried oregano

This aromatic herb batter gives the aubergine slices a light, crisp and golden coating. Salting the aubergines before cooking prevents them absorbing too much oil when they are fried.

1 Make the batter: sift the flour and baking powder into a bowl and beat in the egg and olive oil with a little water. Gradually beat in the remaining water until you have a smooth lump-free batter. Stir in the oregano. Alternatively, you can make it in a food processor by blending all the ingredients together. Transfer to a bowl and set aside for 30 minutes.

2 Cut the stalk ends off the aubergines and discard. Cut the aubergines lengthways into 1cm (½in) thick slices. Place the slices in a large colander and sprinkle with salt. Leave for 30 minutes to exude their juice. Rinse under cold running water and pat dry with kitchen paper (paper towels).

3 Place a large frying pan (skillet) over a low to medium heat. Add enough olive oil to give a depth of 5mm (¼in). When it's really hot, dip some aubergine slices into the batter to coat them all over and add to the pan in a single layer. Fry for 2–3 minutes until golden and crisp underneath, then turn them over and fry the other side. Remove from the pan and drain on kitchen paper. Keep warm while you cook the remaining fritters in the same way.

4 Serve the hot fritters sprinkled with sea salt and drizzled with honey with some lemon wedges on the side for squeezing over.

OR YOU CAN TRY THIS...
– Add some courgette slices to the batter and fry with the aubergines.
– Serve with skordalia (Greek garlic sauce), aioli, tzatziki or hummus.
– If you're in a hurry, just dip the aubergine slices in seasoned flour and fry as above.

MOUTABAL

SERVES: 4 | **PREP:** 15 MINUTES | **COOK:** 25–40 MINUTES

2 large aubergines
  (eggplants)
2 tbsp tahini, plus extra
2 garlic cloves, crushed
juice of 1 lemon, plus extra
1 tbsp olive oil, plus extra
  for sprinkling
a pinch of ground cumin
smoked paprika, for dusting
2 tbsp toasted pine nuts
a few sprigs of flat-leaf
  parsley, chopped
sea salt
warm pitta or flatbreads,
  to serve

This aubergine dip is made with tahini and is the smokier Lebanese version of the classic baba ganoush. It's very important to char the aubergines before oven-roasting them, to bring out their distinctive smoky flavour.

1 Preheat the oven to 180°C, 350°F, gas mark 4.

2 Slash each aubergine 3–4 times with a sharp knife. Place them over a gas flame on top of the hob (stove) or on a oiled barbecue or hot griddle (grill) pan for 5–10 minutes until the skins are charred and they are soft inside. Turn them often with hot tongs, taking care not to burn yourself.

3 Put the aubergines on a lightly oiled baking tray (cookie sheet) and cook in the preheated oven for 20–30 minutes until they are really soft. Remove from the oven and set aside to cool.

4 When they are cool enough to handle, peel off the skin and mash the aubergine flesh in a bowl with a fork. Add the tahini, garlic, lemon juice and olive oil and beat together well until everything is thoroughly combined. Season to taste with salt, then add the cumin plus more lemon juice or tahini, if needed.

5 Spoon the moutabal into a shallow serving dish and sprinkle with olive oil. Dust with smoked paprika and sprinkle the pine nuts and parsley over the top. Serve with warm pitta or flatbreads.

OR YOU CAN TRY THIS...

– Instead of beating the moutabal by hand you can blitz everything in a food processor, but the texture will be creamier.
– For a spicier version, add a pinch of cayenne pepper or chilli powder.
– Substitute chopped mint, basil or coriander (cilantro) for the parsley.
– Sprinkle with sumac before serving.

MELITZANOSALATA

SERVES: 4 | **PREP:** 10 MINUTES | **DRAIN:** 30 MINUTES | **COOK:** 1 HOUR

2 large aubergines
  (eggplants)
4 garlic cloves, peeled
1 tbsp fresh white
  breadcrumbs
60ml/2fl oz (¼ cup)
  olive oil
juice of ½ lemon or 1 tbsp
  red wine vinegar
sea salt and freshly ground
  black pepper
a handful of flat-leaf parsley,
  chopped
warm pitta bread or garlic
  toast, to serve

Throughout Greece, this traditional aubergine dip is often served as part of the meze selection of small dishes before a meal. It's great eaten with thick slices of toast and a juicy tomato salad or some griddled squid or octopus. It's less sophisticated and simpler to make than moutabal or baba ganoush.

1 Preheat the oven to 180°C, 350°F, gas mark 4. Line a baking tray (cookie sheet) with baking parchment (parchment paper).

2 Put the aubergines on the lined baking tray and bake in the preheated oven for 1 hour until they are soft. Remove from the oven and set aside until cool.

3 Carefully peel away the skin over a colander, letting the flesh drop into the colander below. Leave for 30 minutes to drain away any bitter juice.

4 Transfer to a food processor and add the garlic, breadcrumbs and olive oil. Blitz until smooth.

5 Next, season to taste with salt and pepper and add a little lemon juice or vinegar, adjusting to taste.

6 Serve sprinkled with parsley with warm pitta bread triangles or garlic toast.

OR YOU CAN TRY THIS...
– Sprinkle with olive oil and lemon juice before serving.
– If you love garlic, do as the Greeks do and add 2–3 more cloves.
– Add some grated onion or diced tomato.
– For a creamier dip, stir in some plain Greek yoghurt.
– Garnish with finely sliced spring onions (scallions) or some chopped mint or basil.

AUBERGINE & ROASTED RED PEPPER DIP

SERVES: 4 | **PREP:** 10 MINUTES | **COOK:** 25–35 MINUTES

2 large aubergines
  (eggplants)
2 red (bell) peppers
olive oil, for brushing
3 garlic cloves, crushed
½ tsp smoked paprika
a pinch of ground cumin
juice of ½ lemon
200g/7oz (scant 1 cup)
  0%-fat Greek yoghurt
a handful of dill or flat-leaf
  parsley, chopped
sea salt and freshly ground
  black pepper
warm pitta or flatbreads,
  to serve

This creamy, colourful dip has the distinctive smoky flavour of aubergines, enhanced by the addition of smoked paprika. Serve as a dip or spread on toast or warm pitta bread and sprinkle with herbs or dukkah.

1 Preheat the oven to 180°C, 350°F, gas mark 4.

2 Hold the aubergines and peppers over a gas flame on top of the hob (stove) or place on an oiled barbecue or hot griddle (grill) pan for 5–10 minutes until the skins are charred and they are starting to soften. Turn them often with hot tongs, taking care not to burn yourself.

3 Put the aubergines and peppers on a lightly oiled baking tray (cookie sheet) and cook in the preheated oven for 20–30 minutes until really tender. Remove from the oven and set aside to cool.

4 Discard the aubergine skins and place the flesh in a food processor. Skin and deseed the peppers, removing the stalks and white ribs. Put the flesh in the food processor.

5 Add the garlic, paprika, cumin and lemon juice, and blitz until smooth. Season with salt and pepper to taste and stir in the yoghurt.

6 Serve, sprinkled with chopped herbs, with warm pitta slices or flatbreads.

OR YOU CAN TRY THIS...
– Sprinkle with chopped basil or coriander (cilantro).
– Instead of using the herbs as a garnish, stir them into the dip with the yoghurt.
– Use sweet paprika instead of smoked for a less smoky flavour.
– Add some heat with a diced red chilli or some crushed chilli flakes.
– Or add a dash of fiery harissa paste.
– Add a spoonful of tahini or a little tomato purée (paste).

BABA GANOUSH WITH SEEDY FLATBREADS

SERVES: 4 | **PREP:** 20 MINUTES | **DRAIN:** 30 MINUTES | **COOK:** 20–25 MINUTES

2 large aubergines
(eggplants)
2 garlic cloves, crushed
juice of 1 lemon
2 tbsp olive oil, plus extra
for drizzling
a few sprigs of flat-leaf
parsley or mint, chopped
sea salt and freshly ground
black pepper
pomegranate seeds,
for sprinkling

For the seedy flatbreads:
225g/8oz (1½ cups)
self-raising flour, plus
extra for kneading
½ tsp baking powder
a pinch of salt
½ tsp cumin seeds
½ tsp fennel seeds
225g/8oz (1 cup)
Greek yoghurt
olive oil, for brushing

Smoky aubergine purée is served as a starter throughout the Levant, Greece, Turkey and Egypt, albeit with different names. There are many variations, but this is the classic dish.

1 Hold the aubergines over a gas flame on top of the hob (stove) or place on an oiled barbecue or hot griddle (grill) pan for 5–10 minutes until the skins are charred and they are starting to soften. Turn them often with hot tongs, taking care not to burn yourself. Set aside to cool.

2 Cut the aubergines in half and scoop out the soft flesh into a colander suspended over a bowl, discarding the skin. Set aside for 30 minutes to let any excess liquid drain away.

3 Transfer the drained aubergine flesh to a bowl and mash with a fork. Stir in the garlic, lemon juice, olive oil and herbs. Season to taste with salt and pepper.

4 Next make the seedy flatbreads: mix together the flour, baking powder, salt and seeds in a bowl. Stir in the yoghurt to make a soft dough. Turn it out onto a floured board and knead well. Cut the dough into 4 portions and roll each one out into a thin circle.

5 Brush a griddle pan lightly with oil and set over a medium to high heat. Add a dough circle to the hot pan and cook for about 2 minutes until it turns golden underneath. Flip it over and cook the other side. Keep warm while you cook the remaining flatbreads in the same way.

6 Serve the baba ganoush, drizzled with olive oil and sprinkled with pomegranate seeds, with the warm seedy flatbreads.

OR YOU CAN TRY THIS...
– Add a little tahini to the baba ganoush.
– For a spicy flavour, stir in a pinch of ground cumin or chilli powder, or even some toasted cumin seeds.

CHEESY PESTO AUBERGINE ROLLS

SERVES: 4 | **PREP:** 10 MINUTES | **COOK:** 15 MINUTES

2 large aubergines
(eggplants), trimmed
olive oil, for brushing
150g/5oz creamy
goat's cheese
6 dates, stoned (pitted)
and chopped
1–2 tbsp green pesto
sea salt and freshly ground
black pepper
clear honey or balsamic
vinegar, for drizzling

Aubergine rolls make a delicious starter or party snack. The aubergines can be cooked in advance, then heated and filled just before serving. If you like, you can secure them with wooden cocktail sticks (toothpicks) to prevent them unravelling.

1 Preheat the oven to 200°C, 400°F, gas mark 6. Line 2 baking trays (cookie sheets) with baking parchment (parchment paper).

2 Cut the aubergines lengthways into thin slices. Brush each slice lightly with oil on both sides and place them on the baking trays. Season with salt and pepper. Cook in the preheated oven for about 15 minutes, until tender and golden brown.

3 Meanwhile, mix together the goat's cheese and chopped dates.

4 Cool the aubergine slices slightly, then spread a little pesto over each and put a spoonful of the goat's cheese mixture on one end. Fold the aubergine over it and roll up along its length.

5 Divide the aubergine rolls among 4 serving plates, drizzle with honey or balsamic vinegar and serve immediately.

OR YOU CAN TRY THIS...
– Instead of goat's cheese, use crumbled salty feta mixed with a little Greek yoghurt until creamy.
– Fill the aubergine rolls with finely chopped tomatoes, ricotta and basil or ricotta, spinach and nutmeg.
– Fry or grill (broil) some bacon until crisp and crumble into the cheesy mixture before rolling up.
– Add some griddled red or yellow (bell) pepper slices.
– Drizzle with balsamic glaze or even some soy sauce.
– Serve with oven-baked figs drizzled with honey.
– For a more substantial dish, fill the aubergine rolls with a minced (ground) beef ragu and grated Parmesan.

AUBERGINE, RICOTTA & PEPPER PARCELS

SERVES: 4 | **PREP:** 15 MINUTES | **COOK:** 15 MINUTES

2 large aubergines
   (eggplants), trimmed
olive oil, for brushing
2 bottled roasted red
   (bell) peppers, drained
   and diced
6 stoned (pitted) black
   olives, diced
200g/7oz ricotta
grated zest of 1 lemon
a few sprigs of basil,
   chopped
sea salt and freshly ground
   black pepper
lemon juice and balsamic
   vinegar, for drizzling
snipped chives,
   for sprinkling
8 cocktail sticks
   (toothpicks)

Serve these little parcels as a party dish or first course. You can prepare them in advance and chill them in the fridge until you're ready to eat.

1 Preheat the oven to 200°C, 400°F, gas mark 6. Line 2 baking trays (cookie sheets) with baking parchment (parchment paper).

2 Cut each aubergine lengthways into 8 slices. Brush lightly with oil and place them on the baking trays. Season with salt and pepper. Cook in the preheated oven for about 15 minutes, until tender and golden brown. Remove from the oven and cool.

3 Meanwhile, mix together the red peppers, olives, ricotta, lemon zest and basil. Season to taste.

4 Take an aubergine slice and lay it out flat. Put another slice on top to form a cross. Place a spoonful of the ricotta mixture in the centre where the two slices meet, and fold the ends of the aubergine over the filling to form a neat parcel. Secure with a cocktail stick (toothpick). Repeat with the remaining aubergine slices and filling to make 8 parcels.

5 Put 2 aubergine parcels on each serving plate and drizzle them with a little lemon juice and balsamic vinegar. Sprinkle with chives and serve.

OR YOU CAN TRY THIS...

– Use crumbled feta and yoghurt instead of ricotta, or even
   some mascarpone.
– Use spicy bottled peppers or add some diced fresh chilli or
   a dash of hot sauce.
– If you don't like peppers, use cherry or baby plum tomatoes instead.
– Add some crunchy pine nuts or diced spring onions (scallions)
   to the filling.
– Vary the herbs: try chopped flat-leaf parsley, thyme, oregano or mint.
– Drizzle with truffle-infused balsamic glaze or some lemony vinaigrette.
– Fill with leftover cold risotto.

CHARGRILLED AUBERGINE SLICES WITH SALSA VERDE

SERVES: 4 | **PREP:** 10 MINUTES | **COOK:** 15–20 MINUTES

3 large aubergines
    (eggplants), trimmed
olive oil, for brushing
sea salt and freshly ground
    black pepper

For the salsa verde:
2 cornichons (mini gherkins)
1 tbsp capers
3 anchovy fillets in oil,
    drained
2 small garlic cloves, peeled
a handful of flat-leaf parsley
a few sprigs of dill
a few sprigs of mint
4 tbsp fruity olive oil
1 tbsp red wine vinegar
grated zest and juice of
    1 lemon
2 tsp Dijon mustard

The fresh green salsa verde perfectly complements the subtle smoky flavour of the aubergine slices. Instead of chargrilling them on a hot griddle (grill) pan you can cook them on a barbecue for about 5 minutes on each side.

1 Make the salsa verde: put the cornichons, capers, anchovies, garlic cloves and all the herbs in a food chopper or food processor and blitz to a green paste. Add the oil, vinegar, lemon zest and juice and mustard and blitz again. If it's too thick to drizzle, add a little water to thin it to the desired consistency. Set aside.

2 Cut each aubergine lengthways into 4 thick slices and brush them with oil on both sides. Season lightly with salt and pepper.

3 Place a large ridged griddle (grill) pan over a medium to high heat and when it's hot, add some aubergine slices (you'll have to do this in batches). Cook the slices for 2–3 minutes until charred, golden brown and attractively striped underneath, then turn them over and cook the other side. Drain on kitchen paper (paper towels) and keep warm while you cook the remaining slices in the same way.

4 Divide the griddled aubergine slices among 4 serving plates. Drizzle with the salsa verde and serve warm.

– Vary the herbs in the salsa verde: add some tarragon, chervil, coriander (cilantro) or basil.
– Use white wine vinegar instead of red.
– Add some rocket (arugula) or some torn kale.
– Serve with some hot sauce, e.g. harissa or Sriracha.

**ALTERNATIVE
DRESSING:**

CHERMOULA

SERVES: 4 | **PREP:** 5 MINUTES

This North African green dressing adds heat and spice to chargrilled or roasted aubergine slices. Just drizzle it over and serve scattered with fresh chopped herbs.

2 garlic cloves, peeled
1 small bunch of mint
1 small bunch of coriander
   (cilantro)
1 tsp ground cumin
1 tsp ground coriander
1 tsp sweet paprika
a pinch of powdered saffron
   or saffron strands
a pinch of sea salt
1 tsp harissa
juice of ½ lemon
60ml/2fl oz (¼ cup)
   fruity olive oil

1 Put the garlic cloves, fresh herbs, ground spices, saffron, salt and harissa in a blender, food chopper or food processor and blitz to a paste.

2 Add the lemon juice and olive oil and pulse until you have a smooth dressing.

SWEET & SOUR FRIED AUBERGINE SLICES

SERVES: 4 | **PREP:** 10 MINUTES | **COOK:** 10–15 MINUTES

30g/1oz (scant ¼ cup)
    sesame seeds
2 large aubergines
    (eggplants), trimmed
flour, for dusting
2 tbsp olive or sesame oil

For the sweet and
    sour dressing:
2 tbsp tahini
1 tbsp mirin
1 tbsp soy sauce
1 tbsp rice vinegar
1 tbsp water
2 tsp sugar

This delicious way of serving aubergines combines a Japanese-style sesame dressing with Mediterranean tahini (sesame paste) to create an *agrodolce* (sweet and sour) starter. To make it more substantial, serve it with chicken or lamb and some rice as a main course.

1 Make the sweet and sour dressing: mix all the ingredients together in a bowl until well blended. Taste and adjust the seasoning if necessary by adding more soy sauce or sugar.

2 Heat a small dry frying pan (skillet) over a medium heat, then add the sesame seeds. Toast, tossing gently, for 1–2 minutes until golden and they release their aroma. Remove from the pan and set aside.

3 Cut the aubergines lengthways into thin slices and dust them lightly with flour.

4 Heat the oil in a large non-stick frying pan set over a medium to high heat. Add the aubergine slices, in batches, and cook for about 2 minutes each side until tender and golden. Remove and drain on kitchen paper (paper towels).

5 Serve the aubergine slices drizzled with the sweet and sour dressing and sprinkled with the toasted sesame seeds.

OR YOU CAN TRY THIS...
– Add some sultanas (seedless golden raisins) to the dressing.
– Fry some fresh figs in olive oil and serve with the aubergines.
– Scatter with toasted pine nuts.
– Serve on a bed of salad leaves, e.g. rocket (arugula) or watercress.

FAKON (AUBERGINE 'BACON')

SERVES: 6 | **PREP:** 10 MINUTES | **COOK:** 30 MINUTES

1 large aubergine (eggplant), trimmed
2 tbsp olive oil
2 tbsp soy sauce
1 tbsp apple cider vinegar
2 tbsp maple syrup
2 tsp liquid smoke
1 tsp smoked paprika
a pinch of garlic powder
a pinch of sea salt
freshly ground black pepper

For vegetarians, especially vegans, using aubergines as an alternative to bacon is a no-brainer. The thin and crispy slices taste delicious and are easy to prepare. What's more, you can adjust the ingredients to vary the flavour, depending on whether you want savoury, smoky, spicy or sweet. Eat fakon with eggs for breakfast, in sandwiches or chopped and sprinkled over salads.

1 Preheat the oven to 120°C, 250°F, gas mark ½. Line a large baking tray (cookie sheet) with baking parchment (parchment paper).

2 Cut the aubergine in half lengthways and then cut each half into long thin strips, about 3mm (⅛in) thick. Use a mandolin, if you have one, for the best results.

3 In a bowl, mix together the oil, soy sauce, vinegar, maple syrup, liquid smoke, paprika, garlic powder and salt. Add a good grind of black pepper.

4 Brush the aubergine slices with this mixture (on both sides) and arrange them on the lined baking tray. Don't overlap them – leave a little space in between so they crisp up nicely. You may need 2 baking trays if they won't all fit onto one.

5 Bake in the preheated oven for about 30 minutes (it might take longer depending on your oven and the thickness of the slices) or until crisp and well browned. Remove and cool slightly – the fakon will crisp up even more as it cools.

NOTE: The fakon will keep well for up to 5 days if stored in a sealed container in the fridge.

OR YOU CAN TRY THIS...
– For a less smoky flavour, omit the liquid smoke.
– Add a few drops of vegan Worcestershire sauce.
– Use agave instead of maple syrup.
– Substitute tamari for soy sauce.
– Use with lettuce, tomato and spicy Sriracha mayo in a BLT sandwich.

AUBERGINE POLPETTE WITH TOMATO CHILLI JAM

SERVES: 4 | **PREP:** 30 MINUTES | **COOK:** 1¼ HOURS

2 tbsp olive oil, plus extra
for frying
2 large aubergines
(eggplants), trimmed,
peeled and chopped
85g/3oz (1½ cups) fresh
white breadcrumbs
2 garlic cloves, crushed
a handful of basil, chopped
a handful of mint, chopped
60g/2oz (generous ½ cup)
grated Parmesan cheese
1 medium free-range egg,
beaten
sea salt and freshly ground
black pepper

For the tomato chilli jam:
500g/1lb 2oz ripe tomatoes
2 garlic cloves, peeled
2.5cm/1in piece fresh
root ginger, peeled
and chopped
2 large red chillies,
deseeded and halved
2 tbsp nam pla
(Thai fish sauce)
300g/10oz (scant 1½ cups)
granulated sugar
120ml/4fl oz (½ cup)
red wine vinegar

Make the tomato chilli jam in advance, as it will keep well stored in a cool dry place for up to 12 months. This makes more than enough to accompany the polpette. Once opened, store in the fridge.

1 Make the tomato chilli jam: put half the tomatoes in a food processor with the garlic cloves, ginger, chillies and nam pla. Blitz to a purée, then transfer to a large heavy-based saucepan. Chop the remaining tomatoes into small pieces and set aside.

2 Add the sugar and vinegar to the pan. Stir over a low to medium heat until the sugar dissolves, then turn up the heat and bring to the boil. Reduce the heat, add the reserved chopped tomatoes. Simmer for 30–45 minutes, stirring occasionally, until the mixture reduces and thickens. Pour the hot jam into sterilised jars, cover with a lid and leave to cool.

3 Make the polpette: heat the oil in a large frying pan (skillet) set over a low heat. Add the aubergine and cook, stirring occasionally, for 6–8 minutes until tender. Tip it into a sieve and press gently to squeeze out any moisture.

4 Mix the aubergine with the breadcrumbs, garlic, herbs and grated cheese in a bowl. Stir in the beaten egg until the mixture binds together. Season with salt and pepper. Using your hands, shape the mixture into small balls.

5 Heat some oil in a large frying pan (skillet) set over a medium heat. When the pan is hot, add the polpette and fry, turning occasionally, for about 5 minutes until crisp and golden brown. Drain on kitchen paper (paper towels).

6 Serve the polpette immediately with the tomato chilli jam.

LIGHT MEALS
& SALADS

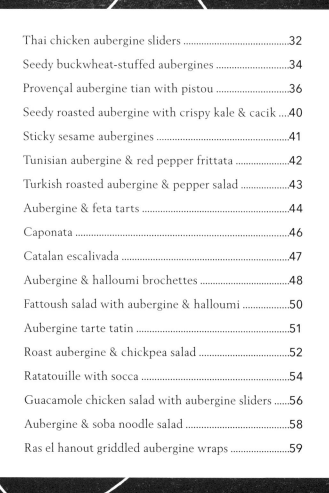

THAI CHICKEN AUBERGINE SLIDERS

SERVES: 4 | **PREP:** 20 MINUTES | **CHILL:** 15 MINUTES | **COOK:** 20 MINUTES

500g/1lb 2oz skinned
    chicken breast fillets
1 red onion, diced
1 red chilli, deseeded
    and diced
3 garlic cloves, crushed
1 tsp grated fresh root ginger
1 stalk lemongrass, peeled
    and finely sliced
grated zest and juice
    of 1 lime
a handful of fresh
    coriander (cilantro)
flour, for dusting
1 large aubergine (eggplant),
    trimmed
olive oil, for brushing
120g/4oz (½ cup) 0%-fat
    Greek yoghurt
¼ small cucumber, diced
sea salt and freshly ground
    black pepper
Thai sweet chilli sauce,
    to serve
crisp salad leaves, to serve

Using roasted or griddled aubergine slices instead of burger buns is the latest food trend. They taste delicious and are light and healthy. These chicken burgers are flavoured with Thai spices and served with cooling yoghurt.

1 Preheat the oven to 200°C, 400°F, gas mark 6.

2 Blitz the chicken, red onion, chilli, 2 of the garlic cloves, the ginger, lemongrass, lime zest and coriander in a food processor until well combined. Season lightly with salt and pepper. With lightly floured hands, divide the mixture into 4 equal-sized portions and shape into burgers. Cover and chill in the fridge for at least 15 minutes to firm them up.

3 Cut the aubergine horizontally into 8 round slices, about 1cm (½in) thick. Place them on a baking tray (cookie sheet) lined with foil and brush lightly with olive oil. Season with a little salt and pepper. Bake in the preheated oven for 7–8 minutes, then turn them over and cook for another 7–8 minutes until tender, golden brown and starting to crisp.

4 Meanwhile, cook the burgers in an oiled griddle (grill) pan or under a preheated hot grill (broiler) for about 8 minutes each side, until thoroughly cooked and golden brown.

5 Mix together the yoghurt, lime juice, cucumber and the remaining crushed garlic clove. Season to taste.

6 Assemble the sliders: place a baked aubergine slice on each serving plate and top with a chicken burger and a spoonful of the yoghurt mixture. Drizzle with chilli sauce and cover with another aubergine slice. Serve immediately with salad.

OR YOU CAN TRY THIS...

- Substitute a pinch of paprika or cumin and some parsley for the chilli, ginger, lemongrass and coriander.
- Use lemon juice instead of lime.
- Add a grilled (broiled) slice of halloumi to each slider.
- Stack the sliders with grilled portobello mushrooms and sliced tomatoes.
- Add some chopped mint and dill to the yoghurt.

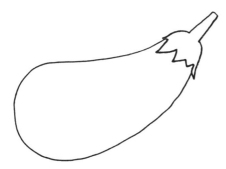

SEEDY BUCKWHEAT-STUFFED AUBERGINES

SERVES: 4 | **PREP:** 15 MINUTES | **COOK:** 30–35 MINUTES

4 medium aubergines
  (eggplants)
3 tbsp olive oil, plus extra
  for drizzling
150g/5oz (1 cup)
  buckwheat
1 small red onion, diced
2 garlic cloves, crushed
3 tomatoes, diced
1 small bunch of flat-leaf
  parsley, finely chopped
125g/4oz (generous
  ¾ cup cup) pine nuts
grated zest and juice
  of 1 lemon
2 tbsp pumpkin or
  sunflower seeds
100g/3½oz feta cheese, diced
sea salt and freshly ground
  black pepper

ALTERNATIVE FILLING:
Mix the scooped-out
aubergine flesh with some
cooked chopped onion and
garlic, herbs, diced tomatoes
and fresh breadcrumbs.
Spoon into the aubergine
shells, top with grated
cheese and bake as above.

These stuffed aubergines taste good served hot, lukewarm or even cold. Eat them with a crisp salad or some griddled chicken for a light lunch on a warm day in summer.

1 Preheat the oven to 200°C, 400°F, gas mark 6.

2 Cut the aubergines in half horizontally through the stalk and place, cut-side up, on a baking tray (cookie sheet). Drizzle with olive oil.

3 Bake in the preheated oven for 20–25 minutes until tender. Remove and set aside to cool – don't turn off the oven.

4 Meanwhile, cook the buckwheat according to the packet instructions.

5 Heat the 3 tablespoons oil in a frying pan (skillet) and cook the red onion and garlic over a low heat for 10–15 minutes, stirring occasionally, until softened. Stir in the tomatoes and parsley and cook gently for 4–5 minutes. Season to taste with salt and pepper.

6 Toast the pine nuts in a dry frying pan set over a low heat for 1–2 minutes, tossing gently, until golden brown and toasted. Remove immediately.

7 Scoop the cooked flesh out of the aubergines and cut into dice. Add to the onion and tomato mixture with the cooked buckwheat, pine nuts, lemon zest and juice, seeds and feta. Stir well and season to taste with salt and pepper.

8 Pile the mixture into the baked aubergine shells and return to the oven for 8–10 minutes. Serve warm or cold with salad.

OR YOU CAN TRY THIS...
– Add a diced chilli or a dash of harissa to the buckwheat filling.
– Omit the feta and sprinkle the stuffed aubergines with grated Parmesan or Cheddar before cooking.

PROVENÇAL AUBERGINE TIAN WITH PISTOU

SERVES: 4 | **PREP:** 20 MINUTES | **SALT:** 30 MINUTES | **COOK:** 1¼ HOURS

2 large aubergines (eggplants), trimmed
1 tsp sea salt
5 tbsp olive oil
2 red onions, thinly sliced
2 garlic cloves, crushed
60ml/2fl oz (¼ cup) red wine
2 large juicy tomatoes, sliced into rounds
leaves stripped from a few thyme sprigs
4 tbsp grated Cantal, Emmenthal or Gruyère cheese
sea salt and freshly ground black pepper
crusty bread and salad, to serve

In Provence a tian is always cooked in a shallow, round earthenware dish, which is unglazed on the outside and glazed inside. Pistou is the Provençal version of the better-known aromatic green pesto sauce, but minus the pine nuts.

1 Preheat the oven to 180°C, 350°F, gas mark 4.

2 Cut the aubergines into rounds, about 1cm (½in) thick, and place in a large colander. Toss them in the sea salt and leave to drain for 30 minutes. Rinse and pat dry with kitchen paper (paper towels).

3 Meanwhile, heat 2 tablespoons olive oil in a frying pan (skillet) set over a low to medium heat and cook the onions and garlic, stirring occasionally, for 8–10 minutes until tender. Stir in the wine and cook for 2–3 minutes, then transfer to a large, shallow, ovenproof baking dish to line the base.

4 Put the sliced aubergines and tomatoes in a bowl with the thyme and remaining olive oil and toss lightly to coat.

5 Arrange the tomatoes and aubergines upright in alternate layers on top of the onions in the baking dish, packing them in tightly. Grind some black pepper over the top and cover loosely with tin (aluminum) foil.

For the pistou:
a large bunch of basil leaves
3 garlic cloves, crushed
a large pinch of salt
60ml/2fl oz (¼ cup) olive oil
60g/2oz (½ cup) grated
    Gruyère cheese

6 Bake in the preheated oven for 45 minutes, then remove the foil, sprinkle the grated cheese over the top and return to the oven for 15–20 minutes until the aubergines are tender and cooked and the top is appetisingly golden brown.

7 Meanwhile, make the pistou: put the basil, garlic and salt in a blender and blitz to a smooth paste. Gradually add the olive oil through the feed tube while the machine is running. Add the cheese and blitz until grainy and well blended. Transfer to a bowl and season with salt and pepper.

8 Drizzle the pistou over the tian and serve lukewarm with bread and salad.

OR YOU CAN TRY THIS...

– Use grated Parmesan for the tian and the pistou.
– Add some sliced courgettes (zucchini) or (bell) peppers.
– Add some baby spinach leaves to the onions for the last 2 minutes of cooking time.
– Sprinkle the warm tian with some good-quality aged balsamic vinegar.
– Sprinkle some breadcrumbs over the top with the cheese.

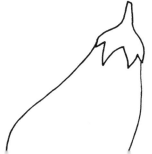

SEEDY ROASTED AUBERGINE WITH CRISPY KALE & CACIK

SERVES: 4 | **PREP:** 15 MINUTES | **COOK:** 25 MINUTES

2 medium aubergines (eggplants), trimmed and cut into chunky matchsticks
4 tbsp olive oil, plus extra for drizzling
1 tsp crushed coriander seeds
30g/1oz (scant ¼ cup) sunflower seeds
½ tsp ground cumin
200g/7oz baby plum tomatoes
300g/10oz kale, stalks removed and roughly shredded
a pinch of dried chilli flakes
aged balsamic vinegar, for drizzling
sea salt and freshly ground black pepper
warm pitta or flatbreads, to serve

For the cacik:
450g/1lb (2 cups) 0%-fat Greek yoghurt
½ cucumber, diced
3 garlic cloves, crushed
a pinch of red pepper flakes, e.g. Aleppo
a handful of mint, chopped

Roasted aubergines can make a delicious warm salad and are surprisingly filling when served with pitta or flatbreads. Cacik is the Turkish version of the Greek tzatziki; it's often thinned with water or lemon juice to make a creamy sauce for grilled (broiled) meat, chicken and whole grains.

1 Preheat the oven to 200°C, 400°F, gas mark 6.

2 Toss the aubergines in the oil and put them in a large roasting tin (pan). Season with salt and pepper, then bake in the preheated oven for 15 minutes.

3 Turn the aubergines over and sprinkle with the seeds and cumin. Add the plum tomatoes, kale and chilli and drizzle with a little oil and balsamic vinegar. Return to the oven for about 10 minutes or until the kale is crisp and the aubergines and tomatoes are tender and charred.

4 Meanwhile, make the cacik: mix together the yoghurt, cucumber, garlic, red pepper flakes and mint. Thin it with 3 tablespoons water and stir until creamy. Season to taste with salt and pepper.

5 Divide the cacik among 4 serving plates, smearing it into a circle. Pile the roasted aubergine, tomato and kale mixture on top. Drizzle with olive oil and serve with warm pitta or flatbreads.

OR YOU CAN TRY THIS...

– Roast some red (bell) peppers or onion wedges with the aubergines.
– Instead of cacik, serve with hummus.
– Omit the cacik and dot the roasted vegetables with goat's cheese or Taleggio for the last 5 minutes of the cooking time.
– Sprinkle some basil, oregano or mint over the vegetables.
– Add some grated lemon zest, flaxseed (linseed), cumin or fennel seeds.
– Substitute dill for mint in the cacik and add some lemon juice instead of water.

STICKY SESAME AUBERGINES

SERVES: 4 | **PREP:** 10 MINUTES | **COOK:** 40–45 MINUTES

4 small aubergines
(eggplants), trimmed
sesame oil, for brushing
5 tbsp teriyaki sauce
4 spring onions (scallions),
shredded
2 tbsp sesame seeds,
for sprinkling
sea salt and freshly ground
black pepper
cooked spinach and steamed
rice, to serve

For the spicy dressing:
1cm/½in piece fresh root
ginger, shredded
1 red chilli, deseeded
and diced
1 garlic clove, crushed
1 tbsp rice vinegar
1 tsp sugar or agave syrup

Aubergines, served Japanese-style like this, make a great vegetarian light meal. Alternatively, you can eat them on their own as a first course without the rice and spinach.

1 Preheat the oven to 190°C, 375°F, gas mark 5. Line 2 baking trays (cookie sheets) with baking parchment (parchment paper).

2 Make the spicy dressing: mix all the ingredients together in a small bowl.

3 Cut each aubergine in half lengthways and then in half again lengthways so you end up with 16 long wedges. Brush them lightly with sesame oil and season with salt and pepper. Arrange, skin-side down, on the baking trays.

4 Bake in the preheated oven for 15 minutes, then remove and brush the cut sides with the teriyaki sauce. Return to the oven for 25–30 minutes until the aubergine wedges are sticky, golden brown and really tender.

5 Divide among 4 serving plates and sprinkle with the spring onions and sesame seeds. Drizzle with the spicy dressing and serve immediately with some spinach and steamed rice.

OR YOU CAN TRY THIS...
– Use soy instead of teriyaki sauce.
– Add some sake or miso.
– Serve on a bed of egg or rice noodles.
– Use toasted sesame seeds for sprinkling.
– Use halved baby aubergines – you'll need 8 of them to serve 4.
– Substitute clear honey for the sugar or agave syrup.

TUNISIAN AUBERGINE & RED PEPPER FRITTATA

SERVES: 4 | **PREP:** 15 MINUTES | **COOK:** 35 MINUTES

4 tbsp olive oil

450g/1lb aubergines (eggplants), trimmed and diced

1 onion, diced

1 red (bell) pepper, deseeded and diced

2 garlic cloves, crushed

100g/3½oz baby spinach leaves

6 medium free-range eggs

1 tsp za'atar

a good pinch of cayenne pepper

a large handful of flat-leaf parsley, chopped

85g/3oz (generous ¾ cup) grated Parmesan

sea salt and freshly ground black pepper

harissa paste and salad, to serve

This subtly spiced frittata is packed with healthy vegetables and is great for lunch or a light supper. Hand the harissa around separately as it is very fiery and some people may find it too hot for their tastes.

1 Heat the olive oil in a large deep frying pan (skillet) on a low to medium heat. Add the aubergines and cook, stirring occasionally, for about 10 minutes until tender and golden brown. Remove and keep warm.

2 Add the onion, red pepper and garlic to the pan and cook, stirring occasionally, for about 8 minutes until softened. Stir in the baby spinach leaves and cook for 1–2 minutes until they wilt and turn bright green. Stir in the aubergines.

3 Meanwhile, beat the eggs and then beat in the za'atar, cayenne, parsley, Parmesan and seasoning to taste.

4 Pour the beaten egg mixture into the pan and stir into the vegetables. Reduce the heat to a bare simmer and cook gently for about 10 minutes until the frittata is set underneath and golden brown.

5 Pop the pan under a preheated hot grill (broiler) for 4–5 minutes to brown the top.

6 Cool slightly – the frittata is best eaten lukewarm. Slide it out of the pan onto a board or plate and cut into 4 wedges. Serve with some harissa paste and salad.

OR YOU CAN TRY THIS...

– Add some diced courgettes (zucchini) or spring onions (scallions).

– Use chopped coriander (cilantro) instead of parsley.

– Substitute grated Cheddar or Gruyère for the Parmesan, or stir in some crumbled feta.

– Use bottled roasted peppers instead of a fresh one.

TURKISH ROASTED AUBERGINE & PEPPER SALAD

SERVES: 4 | **PREP:** 15 MINUTES | **COOK:** 45 MINUTES

3 large aubergines
   (eggplants), trimmed
3 red (bell) peppers
2 green (bell) peppers
2 large tomatoes
5 garlic cloves, crushed
3 tbsp red wine vinegar
5 tbsp fruity green olive oil
sea salt and freshly ground
   black pepper
1 bunch of flat-leaf parsley,
   chopped

This roasted aubergine salad is eaten in Turkey either as a *meze* or as a light meal with bread or meat. You can also serve it as a topping for bruschetta or a sauce for pasta. If you're pushed for time and enjoy the smoky flavour of aubergines, blister the skin by holding them whole over an open flame until they are really burnt. Do the same with the peppers and then chop as directed in the method below.

1 Preheat the oven to 200°C, 400°F, gas mark 6.

2 Put the aubergines and peppers on a baking tray (cookie sheet) and roast in the preheated oven for about 45 minutes until soft. Add the tomatoes for the last 5–10 minutes, when the other vegetables are tender.

3 Remove from the oven and set aside until everything is cool enough to handle. Peel the aubergines and chop them. Peel and deseed the peppers, discarding the white ribs and stems, and chop the flesh. Peel and deseed the tomatoes and dice the flesh.

4 Transfer to a bowl and add the crushed garlic, vinegar and olive oil. Mix well and season to taste. Add more oil or vinegar, if wished, according to taste.

5 Serve lukewarm or cold with hunks of bread and griddled or roast chicken or lamb.

OR YOU CAN TRY THIS...
– Add the juice of a lemon.
– Stir in a little tahini or thick yoghurt.
– Add some sumac for a spicy lemony flavour.
– Sprinkle with toasted pine nuts before serving.
– Instead of dicing the peppers, aubergines and tomatoes, cut them into larger chunks.
– Use chopped mint or coriander (cilantro) instead of parsley.

AUBERGINE & FETA TARTS

SERVES: 4 | **PREP:** 20 MINUTES | **COOK:** 35–40 MINUTES

2 tbsp olive oil, plus extra
for brushing
2 large onions, thinly sliced
2 tsp sugar
1 tbsp balsamic vinegar
1 large aubergine (eggplant),
trimmed
450g/1lb pack puff pastry
(pie crust)
flour, for sprinkling
3 tbsp green pesto
125g/4oz feta cheese, diced
60g/2oz sun blush
(semi-dried) tomatoes,
roughly chopped
sea salt and freshly ground
black pepper
salad leaves, to serve

These individual tarts are easy to make and taste delicious. The smoky aubergine and salty cheese go well with the sweetly caramelised onions.

1 Preheat the oven to 200°C, 400°F, gas mark 6. Line 2 large baking trays (cookie sheets) with baking parchment (parchment paper).

2 Heat the oil in a large frying pan (skillet) set over a low to medium heat. Cook the onions, stirring occasionally, for about 10 minutes until softened. Stir in the sugar and vinegar and increase the heat. Cook, stirring occasionally, for about 5 minutes until really tender and golden brown.

3 Meanwhile, cut the aubergine into round 5mm (¼in) thick slices and brush both sides with olive oil. Set a griddle (grill) pan over a medium heat and cook the aubergine in batches for about 3 minutes each side until tender and browned. Drain on kitchen paper (paper towels).

4 Roll out the pastry on a lightly floured surface and cut out 4 circles, about 12.5cm (5in) in diameter. Place them on the lined baking trays.

5 Spread the pesto over each circle to leave a thin pastry border. Add the onions and cover with the aubergine slices. Top with the feta and sun blush tomatoes and grind some salt and pepper over the top.

6 Bake in the preheated oven for 20–25 minutes until the pastry has risen and is golden brown and the filling is cooked and golden on top. If it's browning too fast, just cover with a little tin (aluminum) foil.

7 Serve hot or lukewarm with some salad.

OR YOU CAN TRY THIS...
– Use filo (phyllo) pastry instead of puff.
– Use sundried or chopped cherry tomatoes instead of sun blush ones.
– Add grated cheese or diced mozzarella instead of feta.

CAPONATA

SERVES: 4 | **PREP:** 15 MINUTES | **COOK:** 50–55 MINUTES

5 tbsp olive oil
500g/1lb 2oz aubergines
   (eggplants), trimmed
   and cubed
1 large onion, chopped
2 garlic cloves, crushed
2 celery sticks, diced
1 red (bell) pepper,
   deseeded and cut
   into chunks
450g/1lb juicy tomatoes,
   skinned and chopped
85ml/3fl oz (generous
   ¼ cup) red wine vinegar
30g/1oz (scant ¼ cup)
   capers
60g/2oz (½ cup) stoned
   (pitted) green olives
60g/2oz (scant ½ cup)
   sultanas (seedless
   golden raisins)
1 tbsp sugar
45g/1½oz (scant ½ cup)
   pine nuts
a bunch of flat-leaf parsley,
   chopped
sea salt and freshly ground
   black pepper
toasted crusty bread, to serve

With its *agrodolce* (sweet and sour) flavours, this classic aubergine dish is the culinary embodiment of Sicily's history combined with the influences of Arab, Turkish and Greek cuisine. The combination of raisins, pine nuts and aubergines is typically Sicilian. Serve this with grilled (broiled) meat or fish or as a topping for bruschetta or crostini.

1 Heat the oil in a large deep frying pan (skillet) or a sauté pan with a lid set over a medium heat. Add the aubergines and cook, stirring occasionally, for about 5 minutes until tender and golden brown all over. Remove with a slotted spoon and drain on kitchen paper (paper towels).

2 Add the onion, garlic, celery and red pepper and cook, stirring often, until softened – 6–8 minutes. Stir in the tomatoes and vinegar, and reduce the heat to a simmer. Add the capers, olives, sultanas and sugar, then stir in the cooked aubergines. Season to taste.

3 Cover the pan and simmer on the lowest possible heat for at least 30 minutes or until the vegetables are really tender and the liquid has reduced and thickened. Check occasionally and if it's too dry, moisten with a little water.

4 Meanwhile, in a small dry frying pan toast the pine nuts over a medium to high heat for 1–2 minutes, tossing them gently, until aromatic and golden brown. Remove from the pan immediately.

5 Stir most of the parsley into the caponata and sprinkle the rest over the top with the toasted pine nuts. Serve lukewarm or even cold with toasted crusty bread.

OR YOU CAN TRY THIS…
– If you like hot food, add a dash of harissa paste or a chopped chilli.
– Stir in some ground cumin for a spicier flavour.
– Stir in the juice of a squeezed lemon at the end.
– Substitute chopped mint or shredded basil for the parsley.

CATALAN ESCALIVADA

SERVES: 4 | **PREP:** 10 MINUTES | **COOK:** 1 HOUR

2 aubergines (eggplants),
 trimmed and halved
1 red (bell) pepper,
 deseeded and cut
 into quarters
1 yellow (bell) pepper,
 deseeded and cut
 into quarters
2 red onions, quartered
4 large ripe tomatoes,
 quartered
2 garlic cloves, crushed
60ml/2fl oz (¼ cup) olive oil
1 tbsp sherry vinegar
a large handful of flat-leaf
 parsley, chopped
sea salt and freshly ground
 black pepper
crusty bread, to serve

This roasted salad is the Spanish version of the Provençal ratatouille. It's widely eaten in Catalunya, either hot with meat, fish or a tortilla, or cold on its own as part of a tapas spread, served with hunks of crusty bread to mop up the juices. This will keep well for 4–5 days if stored in a sealed container in the fridge. You can eat it cold or reheat it.

1 Preheat the oven to 180°C, 350°F, gas mark 4.

2 Put the aubergines, peppers, onions and tomatoes in a large roasting tin (pan). Add the garlic and drizzle the olive oil over the top. Season with salt and pepper.

3 Roast in the preheated oven for 1 hour until the vegetables are really tender. Remove from the oven and leave to cool.

4 When the vegetables are cool enough to handle, cut or tear them into smaller pieces and transfer to a serving dish.

5 Mix the olive oil from the pan with the sherry vinegar and pour over the vegetables. Sprinkle with parsley and serve with crusty bread.

OR YOU CAN TRY THIS...
– Add a green (bell) pepper or use large Spanish onions.
– Make it spicy by adding a pinch of ground cumin or some smoked paprika.
– You can grill (broil) the vegetables over hot coals on a barbecue before dressing with olive oil and vinegar. This gives them a smokier flavour.

AUBERGINE & HALLOUMI BROCHETTES

SERVES: 4 | **PREP:** 15 MINUTES | **MARINATE:** 30 MINUTES | **COOK:** 10–15 MINUTES

1 large aubergine (eggplant),
   trimmed and cut into
   large chunks
2 red onions, cut into wedges
2 red (bell) peppers,
   deseeded and cut
   into chunks
125g/4oz halloumi,
   cut into chunks
120g/4oz (½ cup) hummus
warm pitta or flatbreads,
   to serve

*For the lemon and herb
   marinade:*
5 tbsp olive oil
juice of 1 lemon
1 tbsp capers, diced
2 garlic cloves, crushed
leaves stripped from
   a few oregano sprigs
sea salt and freshly ground
   black pepper

These brochettes are so simple to make and can be cooked under
a hot grill (broiler) or even in a griddle (grill) pan if you don't want
to fire up the barbecue.

1 Make the lemon and herb marinade: beat all the ingredients until
   well blended.

2 Put the aubergine, onions, peppers and halloumi in a bowl and pour
   over most of the marinade – reserve a little for dressing the cooked
   brochettes. Set aside in a cool place for 30 minutes to marinate.

3 Assemble the brochettes: thread the marinated vegetables and
   halloumi alternately onto 4 long or 8 short skewers. If using wooden
   ones, soak them in water first to prevent them burning.

4 Cook on a barbecue or under a preheated hot grill (broiler), turning
   them occasionally, for 10–15 minutes until the vegetables are tender
   and slightly charred and the halloumi is golden.

5 Transfer the brochettes to 4 serving plates and drizzle with the
   remaining marinade. Serve immediately with hummus and warm
   pittas or flatbreads.

OR YOU CAN TRY THIS...
   – Add some cherry tomatoes, courgette (zucchini) chunks or button
     mushrooms to the skewers.
   – Use lemon thyme, parsley or coriander (cilantro) instead of oregano.
   – Serve with tzatziki or some Greek yoghurt.
   – If you're watching your weight, use reduced-fat halloumi.
   – Use green or yellow (bell) peppers instead of red.

FATTOUSH SALAD WITH AUBERGINE & HALLOUMI

SERVES: 4 | **PREP:** 15 MINUTES | **COOK:** 10–12 MINUTES

1 large aubergine (eggplant), trimmed

3 tbsp olive oil

250g/9oz halloumi cheese, sliced

350g/12oz baby plum tomatoes, diced

½ red onion, diced

½ cucumber, diced

a bunch of radishes, trimmed and thinly sliced

2 baby gem lettuces, shredded

1 bunch of mint, chopped

1 bunch of flat-leaf parsley, chopped

4 pittas or flatbreads

For the lemon sumac dressing:

grated zest and juice of 1 lemon

5 tbsp fruity olive oil

1 garlic clove, crushed

1 tbsp sumac

sea salt and freshly ground black pepper

This crunchy Lebanese salad is a great way of using up leftover stale pitta or flatbreads. The aubergine adds a velvety texture while the halloumi makes it more substantial and filling.

1 Slice the aubergine into rounds and brush with some of the olive oil. Heat a griddle (grill) pan over a medium heat and cook the aubergine in batches for about 3 minutes each side until tender and golden brown. Drain on kitchen paper (paper towels).

2 Brush the remaining oil over the halloumi and add to the griddle pan. Cook for about 2 minutes each side until golden brown and attractively striped.

3 Put the tomatoes, onion, cucumber, radishes and lettuce in a large serving bowl and mix together with the chopped herbs.

4 Make the lemon sumac dressing: whisk all the ingredients together in a bowl or shake vigorously in a screwtop jar until well combined.

5 Toast the pitta or flatbreads or heat them in the griddle pan until warm and just starting to crisp. Break them into small bite-sized pieces and add to the salad with the aubergine.

6 Sprinkle the dressing over the top and lightly toss until everything is glistening. Add the halloumi and serve immediately.

OR YOU CAN TRY THIS...

– Sprinkle with toasted cumin or fennel seeds.
– Use spring onions (scallions) instead of a red onion.
– Use chopped basil or coriander (cilantro).
– Use halved cherry tomatoes instead of baby plum ones.
– Add a teaspoon of za'atar or a dash of pomegranate molasses to the dressing.

AUBERGINE TARTE TATIN

SERVES: 4 | **PREP:** 20 MINUTES | **COOK:** 1½ HOURS

3 tbsp olive oil, plus extra for brushing
2 red onions, thinly sliced
2 garlic cloves, crushed
1 tsp brown sugar
1 tbsp red wine vinegar
leaves stripped from a few oregano sprigs
1 large aubergine (eggplant), trimmed
3 tbsp caster (superfine) sugar
30g/1oz (2 tbsp) melted butter
350g/12oz ready-rolled puff pastry (pie crust)
sea salt and freshly ground black pepper
salad leaves, to serve

If you've never considered making a savoury tarte tatin, try this. It makes a delicious vegetarian meal and you can make it in advance and reheat it or even eat it cold later.

1 Heat the oil in a frying pan (skillet) set over a medium heat. Cook the red onions, stirring occasionally, for 10–15 minutes until tender. Stir in the garlic, sugar, vinegar and oregano and cook over a low heat for 20–30 minutes until really soft and golden.

2 Preheat the oven to 180°C, 350°F, gas mark 4. Cut the aubergine into thin rounds and then cut each round in half into a half-moon shape. Brush lightly with oil.

3 Set an ovenproof frying pan or cast-iron round dish over a medium to high heat. Add the caster sugar and cook for about 4 minutes until it melts into a deep golden caramel syrup. Remove from the heat before it gets dark brown and burns. Stir in the butter.

4 Arrange the aubergine half moons in overlapping concentric circles in the pan on top of the caramel. Sprinkle with a little salt and pepper and spoon the red onions over the top.

5 Roll out the puff pastry to a large circle and lay it over the pan or dish so it covers it completely and overlaps the sides. Tuck the edge of the pastry inside the dish around the filling to enclose it. Prick the top with a fork.

6 Bake in the preheated oven for 40–45 minutes until the pastry is risen and golden brown.

7 Place a large serving plate over the top of the pan or dish and invert it carefully, using a cloth to prevent burning yourself, so the plate is underneath and the tart comes out onto it with the caramelised aubergine on top. Allow to cool a little, then cut the tart into wedges and serve lukewarm with salad.

ROAST AUBERGINE & CHICKPEA SALAD

SERVES: 4 | **PREP:** 15 MINUTES | **COOK:** 20 MINUTES

2 aubergines (eggplants),
    trimmed
3 tbsp olive oil, plus extra
    for grilling (broiling)
2 tsp harissa
1 radicchio, trimmed and
    separated into leaves
balsamic vinegar,
    for drizzling
1 x 400g/14oz can
    (1½ cups) chickpeas,
    rinsed and drained
1 small red onion, diced
75g/3oz wild rocket (arugula)
    or baby spinach leaves
a handful of flat-leaf parsley,
    finely chopped
60g/2oz feta cheese,
    crumbled
seeds of ¼ pomegranate

*For the yoghurt and
    tahini dressing:*
240g/8oz (1 cup)
    natural yoghurt
2 tbsp tahini
1 garlic clove, crushed
2 tbsp olive oil
grated zest and juice of
    1 lemon
sea salt and freshly ground
    black pepper

Aubergines are sometimes referred to as 'the poor man's meat', due to their firm texture and ability to make you feel full. This warm salad is a case in point. Here aubergines are paired with chickpeas and feta to create a delicious and satisfying meal.

1 Preheat the oven to 190°C, 375°F, gas mark 5.

2 Make the yoghurt and tahini dressing: mix all the ingredients together in a bowl.

3 Cut the aubergines into thin slices lengthways. Mix the olive oil and harissa and brush over both sides of the slices. Arrange on a baking tray (cookie sheet) and cook in the preheated oven for about 20 minutes until golden brown and tender.

4 Meanwhile, lightly oil a griddle (grill) pan and place over a high heat. Add the radicchio and cook for 2–3 minutes until slightly charred on both sides. Remove from the pan and drizzle with balsamic vinegar.

5 Put the roasted aubergines in a large bowl with the warm radicchio, chickpeas, red onion, rocket or spinach and herbs. Lightly toss everything together and drizzle the yoghurt and tahini dressing over the top. Serve warm, scattered with feta and pomegranate seeds.

OR YOU CAN TRY THIS...

– Add some toasted seeds or chopped hazelnuts and pistachios.
– Use red or white chicory (Belgian endive) instead of radicchio.
– Try using coriander (cilantro) instead of parsley.
– Substitute canned cannellini or butter beans (lima beans) for the chickpeas.
– Add roasted sweet (bell) peppers, courgettes (zucchini) and red onions.
– Serve with griddled halloumi cheese.
– Serve with warm pitta triangles.

RATATOUILLE WITH SOCCA

SERVES: 4 | **PREP:** 20 MINUTES | **STAND:** 1 HOUR | **COOK:** 1¼ HOURS

4 tbsp olive oil
2 onions, thinly sliced
2 garlic cloves, crushed
1 large aubergine
   (eggplant), trimmed
   and sliced
2 large courgettes
   (zucchini), sliced
2 red or green (bell)
   peppers, deseeded
   and sliced
450g/1lb tomatoes,
   skinned and chopped
1 tsp sugar
a few drops of red
   wine vinegar
¼ tsp crushed
   coriander seeds
sea salt and freshly ground
   black pepper
a small handful of basil,
   chopped

These golden socca pancakes are served warm, cut into wedges and topped with ratatouille. Both are specialities of Nice and feature the distinctive flavours, colours and ingredients of Provence. You can serve the ratatouille hot, lukewarm or cold. It also makes a delicious accompaniment to roasted or grilled (broiled) meat, chicken or fish.

1 Preheat the oven to 200°C, 400°F, gas mark 6.

2 Make the socca: sift the flour and salt into a bowl. Whisk in the water until you have a smooth batter. Stir in 2 tablespoons of the olive oil, the rosemary and cumin and leave to stand for 1 hour.

3 Heat the remaining olive oil in a 20cm (8in) ovenproof frying pan (skillet) over a medium heat. Add the onion and cook for 8–10 minutes, stirring occasionally, until tender. Tip the onion into the batter and stir well.

4 While the socca batter is resting, make the ratatouille. Heat the oil in a pan set over a low heat and add the onions and garlic. Cook, stirring occasionally, for about 10 minutes until softened.

5 Add the aubergine, courgettes and peppers, then cover the pan and simmer for 15 minutes. Stir in the tomatoes, sugar, vinegar and coriander seeds. Season with salt and pepper. Cook gently over a low heat for 15–20 minutes until all the vegetables are really tender and the mixture thickens and reduces.

For the socca pancakes:
250g/9oz (scant 2 cups)
    gram flour
    (chickpea flour)
a large pinch of salt
550ml/18fl oz (2¼ cups)
    water
4 tbsp olive oil
leaves stripped
    from 2 rosemary
    sprigs, chopped
a pinch of ground cumin
1 red onion, thinly sliced

6 When the ratatouille is nearly cooked, make the socca pancakes. Pour one-quarter of the batter into a hot ovenproof frying pan and turn up the heat. As soon as it starts to bubble, pop the pan into the preheated oven for about 4 minutes until the pancake is browned underneath. Turn it over and return to the oven for 3–4 minutes until golden brown and crisp on the outside but slightly custardy inside. Remove and drain on kitchen paper (paper towels). Keep warm while you cook the remaining pancakes in the same way.

7 Divide the ratatouille among 4 deep serving plates. Sprinkle with basil and serve with the hot socca pancakes.

OR YOU CAN TRY THIS...

– Sprinkle the ratatouille with chopped parsley.
– Serve with warm flatbreads or hunks of bread if you don't want to make the socca.
– Add some black olives to the ratatouille.

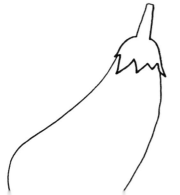
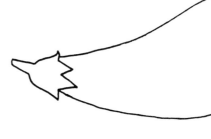

GUACAMOLE CHICKEN SALAD WITH AUBERGINE SLIDERS

SERVES: 4 | **PREP:** 15 MINUTES | **COOK:** 8–12 MINUTES

1 large aubergine (eggplant), trimmed
2 tbsp olive oil
sea salt, to sprinkle
3 cooked chicken breast fillets, skinned
2 juicy tomatoes, diced
a few crisp salad leaves
soured cream and warm tortillas, to serve

For the guacamole:
1 red or green chilli, diced
½ red onion, diced
1 garlic clove, crushed
½ tsp sea salt
2 ripe avocados, peeled and stoned (pitted)
juice of 1 lime
1 small bunch coriander (cilantro), chopped
freshly ground black pepper

Griddled aubergine slices make a healthy and delicious alternative to burger buns. In this Mexican twist on burgers, we've made a spicy guacamole and added chicken for a filling. You can use leftover roast chicken or buy ready-cooked chicken breasts in your local supermarket.

1 Make the guacamole: crush the chilli, onion, garlic and salt in a pestle and mortar. Roughly mash the avocado flesh with a fork and stir in the lime juice. Mix in the coriander and crushed chilli mixture and add a grinding of black pepper.

2 Cut the aubergine into 8 thick rounds and drizzle with the olive oil. Heat a griddle (grill) pan set over a medium heat and add 4 aubergine slices. Cook for 2–3 minutes each side until tender and golden brown. Remove and drain on kitchen paper (paper towels) and sprinkle with sea salt. Cook the remaining aubergine in the same way.

3 Shred or dice the cooked chicken and mix into the guacamole with the diced tomatoes.

4 Assemble the sliders: divide the chicken guacamole mixture into 4 portions. Place some salad leaves on 4 griddled aubergine slices and top with the chicken guacamole mixture. Cover with another aubergine slice and sprinkle with sea salt. Serve immediately with soured cream and warm tortillas.

OR YOU CAN TRY THIS...

– Use finely diced spring onions (scallions) instead of red onion.
– Instead of chicken, use grilled (broiled) large prawns (jumbo shrimp).
– Add some crispy bacon rashers or diced pancetta.
– Roll the aubergine slices, guacamole chicken, salad leaves and soured cream in some large tortilla wraps.
– Serve with hot salsa or pico de gallo for extra heat.

AUBERGINE & SOBA NOODLE SALAD

SERVES: 4 | **PREP:** 15 MINUTES | **COOK:** 20–25 MINUTES

2 aubergines (eggplants), trimmed

4 tbsp olive oil

250g/9oz soba noodles (dry weight)

2 tbsp sesame seeds

1 ripe mango, peeled, stoned (pitted) and cut into chunks

½ cucumber, sliced into long strips

4 spring onions (scallions), shredded

a handful of basil leaves, torn

For the dressing:

5 tbsp soy sauce

3 tbsp rice wine vinegar

2 garlic cloves, crushed

1 red chilli, diced

1 tsp diced fresh root ginger

1 tbsp brown sugar

2 tsp toasted sesame oil

The combination of smoky aubergines, earthy soba noodles and sweet mango tossed in a sesame and ginger-flavoured dressing with some heat from the chilli is a good one. This salad is really easy to make and you can eat it warm or cold the following day for a packed lunch.

1 Preheat the oven to 200°C, 400°F, gas mark 6. Line a baking tray (cookie sheet) with baking parchment (parchment paper).

2 Cut the aubergines into 2.5cm (1in) chunks. Lightly toss them in the olive oil in a bowl and spread them out on the lined baking tray. Roast in the preheated oven for 20–25 minutes until really tender and golden brown.

3 Meanwhile, cook the soba noodles according to the instructions on the packet.

4 Make the dressing: mix all the ingredients together in a bowl until well blended.

5 Toast the sesame seeds in a small dry frying pan (skillet) set over a medium to high heat, tossing them gently for 1–2 minutes until they are golden and fragrant. Remove from the pan immediately before they burn.

6 Put the aubergines, warm noodles, mango and cucumber in a serving bowl. Toss in the dressing and sprinkle with the spring onions, basil and toasted sesame seeds.

OR YOU CAN TRY THIS...

– Add some crumbled feta cheese or cubes of cooked tofu.
– Stir in some sliced radishes or red onion.
– Add the juice of a lime.
– Use a pinch of dried chilli flakes instead of a fresh chilli.
– Try chopped mint or coriander (cilantro) instead of basil.

RAS EL HANOUT GRIDDLED AUBERGINE WRAPS

SERVES: 4 | **PREP:** 15 MINUTES | **COOK:** 20 MINUTES

2 aubergines (eggplants), trimmed

4 tbsp olive oil

1 tbsp ras el hanout

a pinch of sea salt

1 red onion, cut into 8 wedges

4 flour tortilla wraps

a small handful of wild rocket (arugula)

pomegranate molasses, for drizzling

seeds of ½ pomegranate

harissa, to serve

For the sumac yoghurt sauce:
240g/8oz (1 cup) 0%-fat Greek yoghurt

a handful of mint, finely chopped

a few sprigs of dill, chopped

1 tbsp sumac

sea salt and freshly ground black pepper

These wraps are so easy to make and there's virtually no washing up. You can buy the North African ras el hanout spice blend in most supermarkets and delis. It's a fragrant mixture of ground coriander, cumin, cinnamon, ginger, turmeric, cardamom, fenugreek, saffron and rose petals.

1 Make the sumac yoghurt sauce: mix all the ingredients together in a bowl, seasoning to taste with salt and pepper.

2 Cut the aubergines lengthways into 1cm (½in) thick slices. Blend together the olive oil and ras el hanout and brush over both sides of the aubergines.

3 Set a ridged griddle (grill) pan over a medium heat and when it's really hot, cook the aubergines in batches for 3–4 minutes each side until softened, golden brown and slightly charred. Remove and drain on kitchen paper (paper towels), sprinkle with sea salt crystals and keep warm.

4 Add the onion wedges to the griddle pan and cook for 4–5 minutes each side under tender and golden brown.

5 Warm the tortilla wraps in the griddle pan or a low oven.

6 Divide the aubergines and red onion wedges among the warm tortillas. Add some rocket and drizzle with the pomegranate molasses. Spoon the sumac yoghurt over the top and sprinkle with pomegranate seeds. Roll up or fold over the wraps to enclose the filling and serve warm with harissa on the side.

OR YOU CAN TRY THIS...

– Add some griddled baby plum tomatoes or sliced (bell) peppers.
– Sprinkle the griddled vegetables with chopped coriander (cilantro) or flat-leaf parsley.

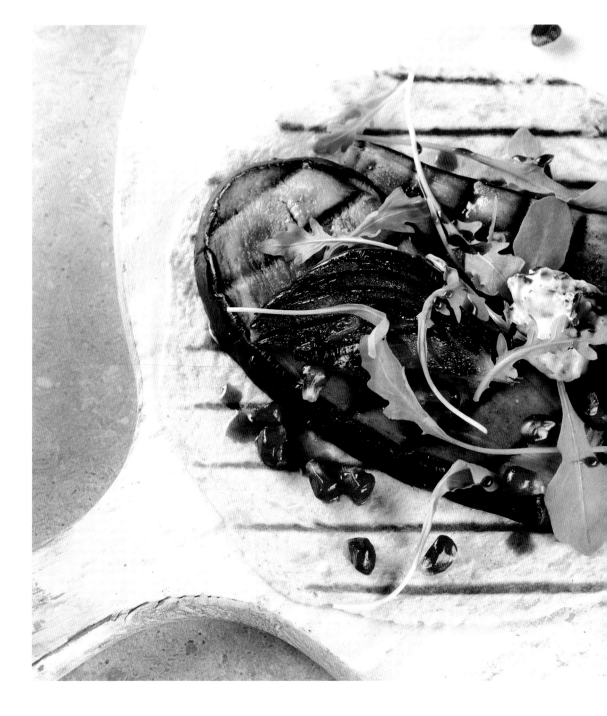

SUPPERS

SPICY INDIAN AUBERGINES WITH RICE

SERVES: 4 | **PREP:** 15 MINUTES | **COOK:** 35–40 MINUTES

5 tbsp vegetable oil
1 large onion, thinly sliced
2 aubergines (eggplants),
    trimmed and
    thickly sliced
1 red chilli, diced
1 red (bell) pepper,
    deseeded and cut
    into chunks
450g/1lb tomatoes, chopped
120ml/4fl oz (½ cup) water
1 x 400g/14oz can
    (1½ cups) chickpeas,
    rinsed and drained
1 small bunch of coriander
    (cilantro), chopped
sea salt and freshly ground
    black pepper
plain yoghurt and steamed
    or boiled rice, to serve

For the spice mixture:
2 tbsp vegetable oil
2 garlic cloves, crushed
2.5cm/1in piece fresh root
    ginger, peeled and diced
2 tsp cumin seeds
1 tsp coriander seeds
2 tsp garam masala
2 tsp paprika
2 tsp ground coriander
2 tbsp tomato purée (paste)
a pinch of sugar

Curries taste even better when you make your own spice mixture. It's quick and easy, and if you make double the quantity, you can store any leftover paste in a sealed container in the fridge for a few days. You need to use quite a lot of oil in this recipe as the aubergines will absorb it as they cook.

1 Make the spice mixture: heat the oil in a frying pan (skillet) set over a low to medium heat. Stir in the garlic and ginger and cook for 1 minute, then add the seeds and ground spices and cook for 1–2 minutes. Stir in the tomato purée and sugar. Fry for 1 minute, then season to taste. Transfer to a blender or food chopper and blitz to a paste.

2 Heat the oil in a large saucepan set over a low to medium heat and cook the onion, aubergines, chilli and red pepper, stirring occasionally, for about 10 minutes until softened. Stir in the spice paste and cook for 1 minute. Add the tomatoes, water and chickpeas.

3 Cook gently for 20–25 minutes until the liquid reduces and the vegetables are tender and fragrant. Check the pan from time to time and add more water if it looks too dry. Taste and add more seasoning if necessary.

4 Sprinkle with coriander and divide among 4 serving plates. Serve with some plain yoghurt and steamed or boiled rice.

OR YOU CAN TRY THIS...
– Use ready-made curry paste, but the result will not be so aromatic.
– For a more creamy sauce, use coconut milk instead of water.
– If you like intense heat, add another chilli.
– Serve with mango chutney or Indian pickles.
– Substitute cucumber raita for the yoghurt.

SICILIAN PASTA ALLA NORMA

SERVES: 4 | **PREP:** 10 MINUTES | **COOK:** 10–12 MINUTES

2 large aubergines
(eggplants), trimmed
100ml/3½ fl oz
(scant ½ cup) olive oil
3 garlic cloves, crushed
1 x 400g/14oz can (2 cups)
chopped tomatoes
a handful of basil leaves,
roughly torn
a good pinch of sugar
500g/1lb 2oz spaghetti
(dry weight)
100g/4oz (1 cup) ricotta
salata, grated
sea salt and freshly ground
black pepper

For the most authentic results, use ricotta salata if you can find it.
It's a salty, hard version of the more familiar ricotta, which is available
in Italian specialist stores and many delis.

1 Cut the aubergines into 5mm (¼in) thick slices. Heat half the olive
oil in a large frying pan (skillet) and fry a batch of the aubergines over
a medium to high heat until they are tender and golden brown on
both sides. Remove and drain on kitchen paper (paper towels) while
you fry the remaining aubergine in the same way, adding more oil as
and when necessary.

2 Meanwhile, heat a little olive oil in another pan and cook the garlic
for 1–2 minutes without browning. Add the tomatoes and simmer
gently until the sauce reduces and thickens. Add most of the basil,
the sugar and some salt and pepper to taste.

3 While the tomato sauce is cooking away, cook the spaghetti
according to the instructions on the packet. Drain, reserving a little
of the pasta cooking water.

4 Return the pasta to the warm pan and gently mix in the tomato sauce
and fried aubergines with one-third of the grated cheese. If it seems
a bit dry, add some of the reserved pasta liquid.

5 Divide among 4 serving bowls and sprinkle with the remaining basil
and cheese.

OR YOU CAN TRY THIS...

– Use grated Pecorino or Parmesan instead of ricotta salata.
– Use peeled fresh tomatoes instead of canned, or half and half.
– Add some heat with a diced deseeded chilli.
– Add a chopped onion with the garlic and cook until softened before
adding the tomatoes.
– Instead of spaghetti, use penne, bucatini, rigatoni or fusilli.

ROSEMARY & LEMON ROAST CHICKEN WITH AUBERGINES

SERVES: 4 | **PREP:** 15 MINUTES | **COOK:** 1¼ HOURS

1 x 1.5kg/3lb whole chicken
1 large lemon, halved
a few sprigs of rosemary
2 large aubergines
    (eggplants), trimmed and
    thickly sliced into discs
5 tbsp olive oil
sea salt and freshly ground
    black pepper

For the herb yoghurt:
240g/8oz (1 cup) 0%-fat
    Greek yoghurt
3 tbsp olive oil
a handful of dill, chopped

A roast chicken is one of the most delicious and easiest meals you can cook. For the best flavour, use a free-range or organic chicken. You can eat this hot, lukewarm or even cold. Serve with roast potatoes, couscous or tabbouleh.

1 Preheat the oven to 200°C, 400°F, gas mark 6.

2 Place the chicken in a large roasting tin (pan) and squeeze the lemon juice over the top. Put the squeezed lemon halves inside the chicken. Strip a few leaves off the rosemary sprigs and sprinkle them over the chicken. Push the stems into the chicken cavity.

3 Arrange the aubergine slices around the chicken and drizzle the olive oil over everything. Grind some sea salt and black pepper over the top.

4 Roast in the preheated oven for 30 minutes, then turn the aubergine slices over in the pan. Return to the oven and cook for 45 minutes until they are really tender and golden and the chicken is cooked and the skin is crisp and golden brown. You can test whether the chicken is cooked by inserting a thin skewer behind a leg – the juices should run clear.

5 While the chicken is cooking, make the herb yoghurt: whisk the yoghurt and olive oil together in a bowl, then stir in the dill and season to taste with salt.

6 Carve the roast chicken and serve with the aubergine slices and some herb yoghurt on the side.

OR YOU CAN TRY THIS...
– Use thyme or oregano instead of rosemary.
– Serve with hummus, skordalia (Greek garlic sauce) or tzatziki.
– Cook the aubergines around a leg of lamb.

THAI GREEN AUBERGINE & PRAWN CURRY

SERVES: 4 | **PREP:** 10 MINUTES | **COOK:** 20–25 MINUTES

2 tbsp groundnut (peanut)
   or vegetable oil
1 red onion, thinly sliced
200g/7oz small Thai
   aubergines (eggplants),
   trimmed and cut into
   quarters lengthways
3 garlic cloves, crushed
2.5cm/1in piece fresh root
   ginger, peeled and diced
1 lemongrass stalk, peeled
   and finely sliced
1 tbsp Thai green
   curry paste
300g/10oz baby plum or
   cherry tomatoes, halved
200ml/7fl oz (scant 1 cup)
   canned coconut milk
4 fresh lime leaves,
   thinly sliced
2 tsp nam pla
   (Thai fish sauce)
400g/14oz shelled raw large
   prawns (jumbo shrimp)
150g/5oz baby
   spinach leaves
1 small bunch of coriander
   (cilantro), chopped
steamed or boiled rice,
   to serve

If you can't find the genuine small green or white Thai aubergines, use any purple baby aubergines or just slice a regular small to medium one and then cut each slice into quarters. The Thai ones tend to be more bitter and strong-flavoured.

1 Heat the oil in a large frying pan (skillet) set over a medium heat and cook the onion and aubergines, stirring occasionally, for 6–8 minutes until softened and golden.

2 Add the garlic, ginger and lemongrass and cook for 1 minute. Stir in the Thai green curry paste and then add the tomatoes. Cook for 2–3 minutes.

3 Add the coconut milk, lime leaves and nam pla and let it bubble away for a few minutes until reduced slightly.

4 Stir in the prawns and spinach. Cook for 2–3 minutes, just long enough for the prawns to turn pink on both sides and the spinach to wilt into the curry and turn bright green. Don't overcook or the prawns will lose their juicy succulence and get tough. Sprinkle with coriander.

5 Serve the curry immediately on a bed of steamed or boiled rice.

OR YOU CAN TRY THIS...

– Omit the prawns (shrimp) and add extra vegetables, such as green beans, butternut squash or (bell) peppers.
– Sprinkle with shredded spring onions (scallions), Thai basil or mint.
– Make the curry with chicken – cook some cubed chicken breast fillets with the onion and aubergines.
– For a hotter curry, add more curry paste or a fresh green chilli.

MOUSSAKA

SERVES: 4 | **PREP:** 15 MINUTES | **COOK:** 1¼ HOURS

3 aubergines (eggplants),
   trimmed and sliced
5 tbsp olive oil, plus extra
   for oiling
1 large onion, chopped
3 garlic cloves, crushed
500g/1lb 2oz (2¼ cups)
   minced (ground) lean beef
1 tsp ground cinnamon
1 tsp dried oregano
1 x 400g/14oz can (scant
   2 cups) chopped tomatoes
150ml/5fl oz (generous
   ½ cup) red wine
a few drops of red wine
   vinegar
a pinch of brown sugar
a handful of flat-leaf parsley,
   chopped
3 tbsp grated kefalotyri cheese
sea salt and freshly ground
   black pepper

For the béchamel sauce:
60g/2oz (¼ cup) butter
60g/2oz (½ cup) plain
   (all-purpose) flour
500ml/18fl oz (generous
   2 cups) milk
2 medium free-range eggs,
   beaten
60g/2oz (½ cup) grated
   kefalotyri cheese

This traditional Greek dish takes a while to make and assemble but it's well worth the effort. If wished, you can double the quantities to make two moussakas and freeze one for later. The aubergines are sometimes fried before layering, but we have baked them to make the finished dish less oily.

1 Preheat the oven to 180°C, 350°F, gas mark 4. Lightly oil 2 baking trays (cookie sheets).

2 Place the aubergine slices on the oiled trays and brush with olive oil. Season with salt and pepper, then bake in the preheated oven for 25–30 minutes until tender and golden brown.

3 Meanwhile, make the meat sauce: heat the remaining oil in a large deep frying pan (skillet) set over a medium heat. Add the onion and garlic and cook, stirring occasionally, for 8–10 minutes until softened. Stir in the beef and cook for a few minutes until browned all over. Add the cinnamon and oregano.

4 Add the canned tomatoes and red wine and simmer gently for at least 15 minutes until the meat is cooked and the sauce has reduced and thickened. It shouldn't be wet. Add the vinegar and sugar, adjusting to taste, and season with salt and pepper. Stir in the parsley.

5 While the meat sauce is simmering away, make the béchamel sauce: melt the butter in a saucepan set over a low heat and stir in the flour to form a paste. Cook for 1–2 minutes and then start whisking in the milk, a little at a time, until smooth. Increase the heat and stir with a wooden spoon until the sauce is thick and smooth. Remove from the heat and whisk in the eggs and then the cheese. Season to taste.

6 Assemble the moussaka: spread one-third of the aubergine slices over the bottom of a large ovenproof baking dish. Cover with half of the meat sauce and then half of the remaining aubergines. Spoon the rest of the meat sauce over the top and cover with another layer of aubergines. Pour the béchamel sauce over and sprinkle with grated cheese.

7 Bake in the preheated oven for 35–45 minutes until bubbling and golden brown.

OR YOU CAN TRY THIS...

– Use minced veal, lamb or pork instead of beef.
– Use fresh tomatoes instead of canned.
– Add some thyme, chopped rosemary or a bay leaf.
– If you can't find kefalotyri cheese, use Parmesan or even some feta.

VEGGIE MOUSSAKA

SERVES: 4 | **PREP:** 15 MINUTES | **COOK:** 1¼ HOURS

3 aubergines (eggplants), trimmed
3 tbsp olive oil, plus extra for brushing
1 large red onion, diced
3 garlic cloves, crushed
300g/10oz mushrooms, sliced
1 x 400g/14oz can (scant 2 cups) chopped tomatoes
1 tbsp tomato purée (paste)
1 x 400g/14oz can (1½ cups) chickpeas, rinsed and drained
a handful of flat-leaf parsley, chopped
sea salt and freshly ground black pepper
2 tbsp grated kefalotyri cheese

This delicious vegetarian moussaka is so simple to make and freezes well. If wished, you can assemble it in advance and leave it for a few hours before baking.

1 Preheat the oven to 180°C, 350°F, gas mark 4. Lightly oil 2 baking trays (cookie sheets).

2 Cut 2 aubergines into thick slices and place them on the oiled trays. Brush with olive oil. Season with salt and pepper, then bake in the preheated oven for 25–30 minutes until tender and golden brown.

3 Meanwhile, heat the olive oil in a large frying pan (skillet) set over a low heat. Cook the onion and garlic, stirring occasionally, for 10 minutes until softened.

4 Cut the remaining aubergine into cubes and add to the pan. Cook, stirring occasionally, for 10 minutes until golden brown. Stir in the mushrooms and cook, stirring, for 3–4 minutes until golden. Add the tomatoes and tomato purée and simmer gently for 10 minutes. Stir in the chickpeas and parsley. Season with salt and pepper.

Continued overleaf →

For the béchamel sauce:
60g/2oz (¼ cup) butter
60g/2oz (½ cup) plain
   (all-purpose) flour
500ml/18fl oz (generous
   2 cups) milk
2 medium free-range eggs,
   beaten
60g/2oz (½ cup) grated
   kefalotyri cheese

5 Make the béchamel sauce: melt the butter in a saucepan set over a low heat and stir in the flour to form a paste. Cook for 1–2 minutes and then start whisking in the milk, a little at a time, until smooth. Increase the heat and stir with a wooden spoon until the sauce is thick and smooth. Remove from the heat and whisk in the eggs and then the cheese. Season to taste.

6 Layer half the aubergine slices in the bottom of a large shallow ovenproof dish. Cover with the aubergine and chickpea mixture and top with the remaining aubergine slices. Pour the béchamel sauce over the top and sprinkle with the grated cheese.

7 Bake in the preheated oven for 35–40 minutes until bubbling and the top is an appetising golden brown.

8 Serve the moussaka with salad – a traditional Greek *horiatiki* of tomatoes, cucumber, onion and feta is great with this.

OR YOU CAN TRY THIS...

– Add some soaked porcini mushrooms to the filling.
– Use canned lentils instead of chickpeas.
– Add a layer of sliced potatoes in the middle.
– Add some Quorn mince or diced tofu.

AUBERGINE RISOTTO

SERVES: 4 | **PREP:** 10 MINUTES | **COOK:** 40–45 MINUTES

6 tbsp olive oil

2 aubergines (eggplants), trimmed and diced

1 onion, diced

3 garlic cloves, crushed

1.2 litres/2 pints (5 cups) chicken or vegetable stock

250g/9oz Arborio or Carnaroli risotto rice

120ml/4fl oz (½ cup) Noilly Prat or other white vermouth

1 tsp saffron strands

grated zest and juice of 1 lemon

a handful of chopped parsley

30g/1oz (2 tbsp) butter, diced

60g/2oz (generous ½ cup) freshly grated Parmesan, plus extra for sprinkling

sea salt and freshly ground black pepper

What elevates a risotto from a tasty meal into a sublimely elegant dish is the quality of the stock used to cook the rice. So don't use a stock cube or a spoonful of bouillon powder, if possible, make some real chicken or vegetable stock or buy a pot of good-quality stock from the deli or supermarket.

1 Heat 4 tablespoons of the oil in a wide heavy-bottomed frying pan (skillet) set over a low heat. Add the aubergines and cook, turning occasionally, for 6–8 minutes until tender and golden brown. Remove from the pan and set aside to cool on kitchen paper (paper towels).

2 Add the remaining oil to the pan with the onion and garlic and cook, stirring occasionally, for about 10 minutes until the onion is really soft but not coloured.

3 Meanwhile, heat the stock in a large pan and keep it simmering gently.

4 Add the rice to the onion and stir well until all the grains are glistening with oil and so hot they begin to crackle. Don't let them colour. Pour in the vermouth and listen for *il sospiro* (the sigh) as a hiss of steam is released. Cook until the liquid has almost evaporated, then add a ladleful of the simmering stock together with the saffron.

5 Continue stirring until all the liquid has been absorbed before adding another ladle of stock. Keep doing this for about 20 minutes until the risotto is thick and the rice grains are plump and swollen but still slightly firm to the bite (al dente).

6 Remove the pan from the heat and stir in the lemon zest and juice and parsley. Season to taste and stir in the butter and Parmesan. Beat the risotto with a wooden spoon until it is really glossy and creamy.

7 Stir in the diced aubergine, then cover and set aside to rest for at least 2–3 minutes before serving sprinkled with Parmesan.

SESAME TOFU & AUBERGINE STIR-FRY

SERVES: 4 | **PREP:** 5 MINUTES | **COOK:** 25 MINUTES

2 tbsp sesame oil
250g/9oz marinated tofu,
    cubed
4 spring onions (scallions),
    sliced
1 red chilli, shredded
2.5cm/1in piece fresh root
    ginger, peeled and diced
8 baby aubergines
    (eggplants), quartered
90ml/3fl oz (generous
    ¼ cup) vegetable stock
2 tbsp dark soy sauce
1 tbsp rice wine vinegar
2 tbsp mirin
2 tsp cornflour (cornstarch),
    plus 2 tbsp cold water
    to mix
juice of ½ lime
2 tbsp sesame seeds
boiled rice or noodles,
    to serve

Like most stir-fries, you can adapt and vary the ingredients in this
dish depending on what you've got in your fridge or store cupboard.
For a non-vegetarian version, use chicken breast fillets instead of tofu.

1 Heat the oil in a wok over a high heat and stir-fry the tofu for
    4–5 minutes until golden. Remove and set aside.

2 Add the spring onions, chilli and ginger and stir-fry for 2 minutes.
    Add the aubergines and cook for 2–3 minutes, then reduce the heat
    to low and add the stock. Cook gently for about 10 minutes until the
    aubergines soften and the liquid reduces.

3 Add the soy sauce, vinegar and mirin and increase the heat to medium.
    Cook for 2–3 minutes and then add the cornflour mix. Stir gently for
    1–2 minutes until the sauce thickens. Stir in the tofu and the lime
    juice, and sprinkle the sesame seeds over the top.

4 Divide among 4 serving bowls and serve immediately with rice
    or noodles.

OR YOU CAN TRY THIS...
– Use fresh firm tofu instead of marinated.
– Add a teaspoon of brown sugar.
– Add some pak choi (bok choy) or baby spinach.
– If you can't get baby aubergines, cut a large aubergine into batons.
– Sprinkle with chopped coriander (cilantro) before serving.

SPICY MOROCCAN CHICKEN & AUBERGINES

SERVES: 4 | **PREP:** 15 MINUTES | **MARINATE:** 15 MINUTES | **COOK:** 40–45 MINUTES

8 chicken thighs
1 red onion, cut into wedges
1 fennel bulb, cut into
    small wedges
1 large aubergine (eggplant),
    trimmed and cubed
300g/10oz baby plum
    tomatoes
1 lemon, cut into wedges
4 garlic cloves, unpeeled
8 dates, stoned (pitted)
2 tbsp red wine vinegar
3–4 tbsp chicken stock
olive oil, for drizzling
3 tbsp toasted pine nuts
a handful of coriander
    (cilantro), chopped
couscous, to serve

*For the spicy Moroccan
    marinade:*
1 tsp coriander seeds
1 tsp cumin seeds
1 tbsp paprika
1 tsp ground cinnamon
2 tsp ground ginger
1 tsp turmeric
1 tbsp honey
2 tbsp olive oil
sea salt and freshly ground
    black pepper

Don't be put off by the long list of ingredients. This is a very simple supper and it's easy to make. You can vary the ingredients depending on what you've got in your fridge and kitchen cupboards.

1 Preheat the oven to 190°C, 375°F, gas mark 5.

2 Make the spicy Moroccan marinade: grind the coriander and cumin seeds in a pestle and mortar. Mix with the other marinade ingredients to make a paste.

3 Slash the chicken thighs with a sharp knife and rub in the spicy paste to coat, then set aside to marinate for at least 15 minutes.

4 Arrange the onion, fennel, aubergine, tomatoes and lemon wedges in a large, shallow ovenproof dish. Tuck the garlic and dates in between and place the chicken pieces, skin-side up, on top. Sprinkle with the marinade, the vinegar and chicken stock. Drizzle with oil.

5 Bake in the preheated oven for 40–45 minutes until the chicken is cooked and golden brown, and the vegetables are tender. Squeeze the garlic out of the skins over the top of the chicken.

6 Serve immediately, sprinkled with pine nuts and coriander, with a bowl of couscous.

OR YOU CAN TRY THIS...

– Use chicken breasts or legs instead of thighs.
– Serve with rice or orzo pasta instead of couscous.
– Spice it up with a dash of harissa or some diced chilli.
– Add sultanas (golden raisins), slices of preserved lemon or fresh apricots.
– Serve with a bowl of yoghurt sprinkled with fresh pomegranate seeds.
– Sprinkle with chopped pistachios and mint.

JAPANESE BLACKENED SALMON WITH AUBERGINES

SERVES: 4 | **PREP:** 15 MINUTES | **MARINATE:** OVERNIGHT | **COOK:** 20 MINUTES

4 x 125g/4oz salmon fillets (skin on)

4 small aubergines (eggplants), trimmed

2 tbsp mirin

1 tbsp soy sauce

3 tbsp white miso paste

1cm/½in piece fresh root ginger, peeled and shredded

1 tbsp caster (superfine) sugar

1 red chilli, deseeded and shredded

2 spring onions (scallions), shredded

steamed rice and Tenderstem broccoli, to serve

For the blackened marinade:

4 tbsp sake

4 tbsp mirin

4 tbsp white miso paste

3 tbsp caster (superfine) sugar

If you enjoy blackened fish in Japanese restaurants, why not try making it yourself at home? It's so easy – just marinate it overnight, then cook it in minutes the following day.

1 Make the blackened marinade: put the sake and mirin in a small pan set over a high heat. Bring to the boil, then reduce the heat and whisk in the miso paste. Stir in the sugar and bring back to the boil, whisking until the sugar dissolves. Set aside to cool.

2 Put the salmon fillets in a shallow bowl and pour the marinade over them. Cover and leave overnight in the fridge.

3 Preheat the oven to 200°C, 400°F, gas mark 6.

4 Cut each aubergine in half lengthways and lightly score a criss-cross pattern on each one with a sharp knife. Arrange them, skin-side down, on a foil-lined baking tray (cookie sheet) and bake in the preheated oven for 15 minutes until tender.

5 Put the mirin, soy sauce, miso, ginger and sugar in a small pan set over a low heat. Stir gently until hot and the sugar dissolves. Spoon over the aubergines and pop them back into the oven for about 5 minutes.

6 Meanwhile, heat a griddle (grill) pan over a medium to high heat and when it's hot add the salmon fillets. Cook for 4–5 minutes each side until the salmon is cooked through and starting to flake.

7 Serve the salmon and aubergines, sprinkled with chilli and spring onions, with some steamed rice and Tenderstem broccoli.

OR YOU CAN TRY THIS...

– Use thick cod fillets instead of salmon.

– Substitute teriyaki sauce or tamari for the soy sauce and use honey instead of sugar, then serve sprinkled with coriander (cilantro).

AUBERGINE & PANEER CURRY

SERVES: 4 | **PREP:** 10 MINUTES | **COOK:** 35–40 MINUTES

4 tbsp vegetable oil, e.g. groundnut (peanut) or sunflower

300g/10oz paneer, cubed

2 medium aubergines (eggplants), trimmed and sliced

1 tsp black mustard seeds

2 garlic cloves, thinly sliced

1 tbsp peeled and diced fresh root ginger

1 tbsp curry powder

675g/1½lb plum tomatoes, chopped

200ml/7fl oz reduced-fat canned coconut milk

1 tbsp garam masala

a handful of coriander (cilantro), chopped

steamed rice and natural yoghurt, to serve

The best paneer to use for this curry is the soft kind with a crumbly, rather than a rubbery, texture, which is similar to ricotta. With its mild flavour, this fresh cheese goes well with spices and is great in vegetarian curries.

1 Heat the oil in a wok or deep frying pan over a low to medium heat. Add the paneer and cook, turning occasionally, for about 5 minutes or until golden all over. Remove with a slotted spoon and drain on kitchen paper (paper towels).

2 Add the aubergine to the pan and cook, turning the slices occasionally, until softened and golden. Stir in the mustard seeds, garlic and ginger and cook for 1 minute, then add the curry powder and cook for 1 minute.

3 Add the tomatoes and coconut milk and simmer gently for 20–25 minutes until the liquid reduces and thickens. If it reduces too much and the aubergines are not really soft, add some more coconut milk or a little water. Stir in the garam masala, paneer and coriander.

4 Serve the curry immediately with steamed rice and a little cooling yoghurt.

OR YOU CAN TRY THIS...

– Cook some thinly sliced onions or shallots with the aubergines.
– Add some drained canned lentils to the curry.
– Vary the spices: try ground cumin, coriander, turmeric and fresh curry leaves.
– Stir in some spinach leaves about 5 minutes before the end of the cooking time.
– Add some lime juice before serving.

MEDITERRANEAN BAKED FISH WITH AUBERGINE

SERVES: 4 | **PREP:** 10 MINUTES | **COOK:** 25–30 MINUTES

4 tbsp olive oil

1 large onion, thinly sliced

1 garlic clove, crushed

1 aubergine (eggplant), trimmed and cubed

400g/14oz ripe tomatoes, chopped

210ml/7fl oz (scant 1 cup) white wine

85g/3oz (generous ½ cup) stoned (pitted) black olives

900g/2lb white fish fillets, e.g. cod or haddock, skinned

juice of 1 lemon

a handful of parsley, chopped

sea salt and freshly ground black pepper

steamed rice or boiled potatoes, to serve

White fish baked with aubergine in a rich tomato sauce is eaten all the year round in Spain, Italy, Greece and southern France. If you don't have fresh fish fillets, use frozen ones.

1 Preheat the oven to 200°C, 400°F, gas mark 6.

2 Heat the olive oil in a flameproof roasting tin (pan) on the hob (stove). Add the onion and cook over a medium heat for 5 minutes until softened. Stir in the garlic and aubergine and cook for 2 minutes, stirring once or twice. Add the tomatoes and wine and let the mixture bubble away for 3–4 minutes.

3 Add the fish fillets and sprinkle with lemon juice. Season with salt and pepper and bake in the preheated oven for 15–20 minutes until the fish and aubergine are cooked and the sauce has reduced.

4 Sprinkle with parsley and divide among 4 serving plates. Serve immediately with rice or boiled potatoes.

OR YOU CAN TRY THIS...

– Add some courgette (zucchini), green or red (bell) peppers or fennel.

– If the tomato sauce is too thick, add a little fish stock.

– Use canned chopped tomatoes instead of fresh.

– Add some chopped dill, basil, oregano or thyme.

– Use capers instead of olives.

– For a more piquant sauce, add a dash of balsamic or red wine vinegar.

– Add some peeled prawns (shrimp).

SICILIAN AUBERGINE PIZZAS

SERVES: 4 | **PREP:** 30 MINUTES | **RISE:** 1–2 HOURS | **COOK:** 45 MINUTES

500g/1lb 2oz (5 cups)
   Italian 00 flour or strong
   white flour, plus extra
   for kneading
1 x 7g/¼oz sachet
   fast-action yeast
1 tsp sea salt
300ml/10floz(1¼ cups)
   warm water
2 tbsp fennel or hemp seeds
stripped leaves from a
   few sprigs of thyme
   or rosemary

These pizzas take a little while to make but are well worth the effort. They are a good example of the Sicilian *agrodolce* (sweet and sour) tradition, with the natural sweetness of the onions and sultanas offset by the acidity of the vinegar.

1 Put the flour, yeast and salt in a large mixing bowl. Make a well in the centre and pour in most of the warm water. Mix to a soft dough, drawing in the flour from the sides with your hand. Alternatively, use a food mixer fitted with a special dough hook. If the dough is too dry, add a little more warm water.

2 Put the ball of dough on a well-floured work surface and knead by hand for 10 minutes until smooth, silky and elastic. Alternatively, use the food mixer.

3 Put the dough in a large lightly oiled bowl and cover with cling film (plastic wrap) or a damp cloth. Leave in a warm place for 1–2 hours until it rises and doubles in size.

4 Meanwhile, make the topping: drizzle the aubergine slices with oil and cook them in batches in a ridged griddle (grill) pan over a medium heat for 2–3 minutes each side until tender and browned. Remove and drain on kitchen paper (paper towels).

5 Heat the olive oil in a large frying pan (skillet) set over a low heat. Add the onions and cook very slowly, stirring occasionally, for about 20 minutes until they are really tender and starting to turn golden and caramelise. Remove from the heat and stir in the pine nuts and sultanas. Season with salt and pepper and add a few drops of balsamic vinegar.

Continued overleaf →

For the topping:
2 medium aubergines
   (eggplants), trimmed
   and cut into rounds
3 tbsp olive oil, plus extra
   for drizzling
4 onions, thinly sliced
4 tbsp pine nuts
85g/3oz (½ cup) sultanas
   (seedless golden raisins)
a few drops of balsamic
   vinegar
120ml/4fl oz (½ cup)
   passata
350g/12oz mozzarella, torn
   into pieces or cubed
sea salt and freshly ground
   black pepper

6 Preheat the oven to 230°C, 450°F, gas mark 8. Knock the dough down with your fist and place on a floured work surface. Knead it lightly, adding the seeds and herbs until they are mixed in well. Cut into 4 equal-sized pieces and roll each one out thinly into a large disc. Place the pizza bases on 4 baking trays (cookie sheets).

7 Spread the passata thinly over them, leaving a 2.5cm (1in) border around the edge for the crust to rise. Divide the onion mixture among the pizzas and top with the griddled aubergines. Scatter the mozzarella over the top and drizzle with olive oil.

8 Cook in the preheated oven for 12–15 minutes until the pizza bases are crisp and the cheese has melted. Serve immediately.

OR YOU CAN TRY THIS...

– Drizzle the cooked pizzas with a little green pesto.
– Use red onions instead of white ones.
– Add some heat with cubed pepperoni, salami or chorizo.
– Break an egg into the centre of each pizza before cooking.
– Mix some baby spinach leaves or rocket (arugula) into the onions

LAMB BURGERS WITH BABA GANOUSH

SERVES: 4 | **PREP:** 15 MINUTES | **CHILL:** 30 MINUTES | **COOK:** 10 MINUTES

500g/1lb 2oz minced
   (ground) lean lamb
1 tsp mustard seeds
2 tsp ground coriander
1 tsp ground cumin
a pinch of ground cinnamon
a handful of flat-leaf parsley,
   finely chopped
olive oil, for brushing
4 pitta breads
1 quantity Baba ganoush
   (see page 20)
sea salt and freshly ground
   black pepper

For the fennel salad:
1 large fennel bulb, trimmed
   and thinly sliced
240g/8oz (1 cup) 0%-fat
   Greek yoghurt
1 tsp fennel seeds
a few feathery fennel fronds
   or herb, chopped

You can make these burgers in advance and leave them in the fridge for several hours or even overnight. If you're throwing a party, divide the mixture into 16 small portions and roll into balls before grilling (broiling). Serve on cocktail sticks (toothpicks) with the baba ganoush as a dip.

1 Put the lamb, mustard seeds, ground spices, parsley and some salt and pepper in a bowl and stir well with a fork.

2 Divide the mixture into 4 portions and shape each one into a patty. Cover and chill in the fridge for at least 30 minutes to firm them up.

3 Meanwhile, make the fennel salad: combine all the ingredients together in a bowl, season with salt and pepper and set aside.

4 Brush the lamb burgers with oil and cook under a preheated hot grill (broiler) for about 5 minutes each side, until golden brown.

5 Heat the pitta breads and make a slit down one side to make a pocket. Put a burger in each one together with some baba ganoush. Serve immediately with the fennel salad.

OR YOU CAN TRY THIS...
– Serve in burger buns instead of pitta, or with flatbreads on the side.
– Spice it up with some harissa paste.
– Use ras el hanout instead of the ground spices.
– Substitute minced beef or pork for the lamb.
– Sprinkle the baba ganoush with some fresh pomegranate seeds.

SZECHUAN-SPICED AUBERGINE WITH EGG NOODLES

SERVES: 4 | **PREP:** 10 MINUTES | **COOK:** 30–40 MINUTES

2 large aubergines
(eggplants), trimmed and
cut into medium rounds
3 tbsp vegetable oil
300g/10oz medium egg
noodles (dry weight)
2 spring onions (scallions),
shredded
a few sprigs of coriander
(cilantro), chopped

For the Szechuan sauce:
1 tbsp vegetable oil
2 tbsp Szechuan chilli
bean paste
2.5cm/1in piece fresh root
ginger, peeled and diced
2 garlic cloves, crushed
a pinch of dried red
chilli flakes
210ml/7fl oz (scant 1 cup)
vegetable stock
2 tbsp water
1 tbsp cornflour (cornstarch)
2 tbsp rice vinegar or
Chinese black vinegar
1 tbsp soft brown sugar

This delicious aubergine dish is typical of spicy Szechuan cuisine. The heat of the chilli complements the delicate flavour of the noodles, the silkiness of the aubergines and sharp sweetness of the sauce.

1 Preheat the oven to 200°C, 400°F, gas mark 6.

2 Arrange the aubergines on a baking tray (cookie sheet) and brush with the oil. Roast in the preheated oven for 30–40 minutes until softened and golden brown.

3 While the aubergines are cooking, make the Szechuan sauce: heat the oil in a wok or deep frying pan (skillet) set over a medium to high heat. Stir-fry the chilli bean paste, ginger, garlic and chilli flakes for 1–2 minutes without browning. Add the stock and cook for 2 minutes. Mix the water and cornflour to a smooth paste and add to the wok. Stir well and cook for 2–3 minutes, stirring until the sauce thickens. Reduce the heat and add the vinegar and brown sugar and cook gently for 3–4 minutes.

4 Cook the egg noodles according to the instructions on the packet.

5 Divide the egg noodles between 4 shallow serving bowls. Top with the aubergine slices and pour the Szechuan sauce over the top. Sprinkle with the spring onions and coriander.

OR YOU CAN TRY THIS...

– Stir-fry some minced (ground) pork or chicken and add to the sauce.
– Use sesame oil instead of vegetable oil to make the sauce.
– Substitute rice noodles for the egg noodles.
– Add 1–2 tablespoons Shaoxing wine or a dash of soy sauce.

SPANISH SWEET & SOUR AUBERGINES

SERVES: 4 | **PREP:** 15 MINUTES | **COOK:** 50 MINUTES

4 tbsp olive oil

1 large onion, very thinly sliced

3 garlic cloves, crushed

2 large aubergines (eggplants), cut lengthways into 1cm/½in slices

4 juicy tomatoes, chopped

2 red (bell) peppers, deseeded and sliced

juice of 1 lemon

210ml/7fl oz (scant 1 cup) vegetable stock

4 tbsp red wine vinegar

60g/2oz (generous ¼ cup) brown sugar

3 tbsp sultanas (seedless golden raisins)

3 tbsp pine nuts

a few sprigs of mint, chopped

For the saffron pilaff:

225g/8oz (1 cup) long-grain rice (dry weight)

420ml/14fl oz (1¾ cups) chicken or vegetable stock

a few strands of saffron

2 tbsp olive oil

4 spring onions (scallions), finely chopped

a handful of flat-leaf parsley, finely chopped

sea salt and freshly ground black pepper

The Moors introduced this sweet and sour combination, together with saffron, to Andalucia in southern Spain in medieval times, and it still survives today in many popular dishes.

1 Heat the olive oil in a large frying pan (skillet) set over a low heat. Add the onion and garlic and then layer up the aubergine slices over the top. Cover with the tomatoes and red peppers, then pour the lemon juice and half the stock over the top. Cover the pan and cook gently for 20 minutes.

2 Meanwhile, heat the remaining stock with the vinegar, brown sugar, sultanas and pine nuts in a small pan set over a low heat. Stir until the sugar dissolves and then simmer for 5 minutes.

3 Pour over the aubergine mixture and simmer for at least 30 minutes until the vegetables are tender and the liquid has reduced. Sprinkle with the mint and set aside to cool a little.

4 While the aubergines are cooking, make the saffron pilaff: put the rice and stock in a pan. Add the saffron and bring to the boil. Reduce the heat, cover the pan and cook gently for 15–20 minutes until most of the liquid has been absorbed. Remove from the heat and leave to stand, covered, for 5 minutes until the rice is cooked, tender and fluffy. Stir in the olive oil, spring onions and parsley. Season to taste with salt and pepper.

5 Serve the aubergines with the saffron pilaff. This is best eaten lukewarm or even chilled on a hot summer's day.

OR YOU CAN TRY THIS...

– Make the pilaff more flavourful by adding diced tomato, (bell) peppers and lemon juice.

– Add some smoked paprika to the aubergines.

– Use a small can of chopped tomatoes instead of fresh ones.

SABIH WITH ROASTED CHICKPEAS

SERVES: 4 | **PREP:** 25 MINUTES | **COOK:** 35–45 MINUTES

2 medium aubergines
(eggplants), trimmed
and cut into 1cm/½in
thick rounds
4 flatbreads

For the roasted chickpeas:
2 x 400g/14oz cans
(3 cups) chickpeas,
drained and rinsed
2 tbsp olive oil
½ tsp fine sea salt
1 tsp chilli powder
1 tsp ground cumin
1 tsp smoked paprika
a good pinch of
cayenne pepper

For the tahini sauce:
100g/3½oz (scant ½ cup)
tahini
5 tbsp water
juice of 1 small lemon
1 garlic clove, crushed
4–5 tbsp olive oil

Sabih is a popular dish in Israel, where it's often eaten as a street food stuffed into warm pitta pockets. This looks complicated because there are so many ingredients, but you can make the chickpeas, zhoug paste and tahini sauce in advance, then the sabih takes no time at all to assemble.

1 Make the roasted chickpeas: preheat the oven to 200°C, 400°F, gas mark 6. Put the chickpeas in a bowl with the olive oil and sea salt and toss lightly with the spices until they are evenly coated. Spread them out in a single layer on a baking tray (cookie sheet) and roast in the oven for 25–35 minutes, turning once or twice, until crisp and golden brown. Leave to cool on the tray.

2 Make the tahini sauce: mix the tahini with the water, lemon juice and garlic until smooth.

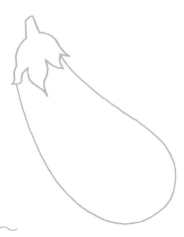

For the zhoug:
1 small bunch of
   flat-leaf parsley
1 small bunch of
   coriander (cilantro)
1 green chilli
½ tsp ground cumin
¼ tsp ground cloves
a pinch of sugar
4 tbsp olive oil
juice of ½ small lemon
2 tbsp water

For the salad:
2 mini cucumbers, diced
2 juicy tomatoes, diced
4 spring onions (scallions),
   chopped
a handful of flat-leaf
   parsley, chopped
2 tbsp olive oil
a good squeeze of
   lemon juice

3 Make the zhoug: blitz all the ingredients in a blender until smooth.

4 Just before you are ready to serve, heat a little olive oil in a large
   frying pan (skillet) and fry the aubergine rounds in batches, adding
   more oil with each batch, until tender and golden brown on both
   sides. Remove from the pan and drain on kitchen paper (paper towels).

5 Mix all the salad ingredients together in a bowl. Warm the flatbreads
   and place one on each serving plate. Spoon a little tahini sauce over
   and then top with the aubergine slices and chickpeas. Drizzle with
   the zhoug and serve the salad on the side.

**OR YOU CAN
TRY THIS...**

– Add some chopped red or green (bell) peppers to the salad.
– Serve with some spicy, hot, Lebanese pickled chillies.
– Use grilled (broiled) or fried field mushrooms instead of aubergines.
– Substitute pittas for the flatbreads.
– Serve with hummus.

SICILIAN AUBERGINE TIMBALE

SERVES: 4 | **PREP:** 20 MINUTES | **COOK:** 45–55 MINUTES

2 large aubergines
(eggplants), trimmed and
thinly sliced lengthways
olive oil, for brushing
225g/8oz pasta, e.g. penne
or bucatini
240ml/8fl oz (1 cup) tomato
sauce (see intro)
150g/5oz mozzarella, cubed
100g/3½oz (1 cup) grated
cheese, e.g. Parmesan,
Pecorino or Grana Padano
a handful of basil leaves,
chopped
sea salt and freshly ground
black pepper
salad leaves, to serve

This aubergine 'pie' is surprisingly easy to assemble and cook. In Sicily and southern Italy, aubergines are often used to encase fillings of pasta or rice – a healthier alternative to pastry (pie crust). You can make the tomato sauce yourself (see page 97) or buy a jar of ready-made sauce in the deli or supermarket.

1 Preheat the oven to 190°C, 375°F, gas mark 5. Lightly oil a deep 23cm (9in) loose-based (springform) tin (pan) or ovenproof baking dish.

2 Brush the aubergine slices with oil and cook under a preheated hot grill (broiler) for 2–3 minutes each side until tender and golden. Drain on kitchen paper (paper towels).

3 Cook the pasta according to the instructions on the packet. Drain well and return to the pan.

4 Add the tomato sauce, mozzarella, most of the grated cheese and the chopped basil. Stir well to distribute the pasta evenly and season with salt and pepper.

5 Line the bottom and sides of the tin or baking dish with the aubergine slices. Make sure they overlap so there are no gaps and let them hang down over the edge of the tin or dish. Fill with the pasta mixture and cover the top with the overhanging aubergine slices to completely enclose the pasta. Sprinkle with the remaining cheese.

6 Bake in the preheated oven for 30–40 minutes until golden brown. Remove and set aside to cool a little.

7 Invert the tin onto a large plate and unclip before serving. If using a dish, invert onto a platter or simply serve straight from the dish. Cut the timbale into slices and eat with salad.

OR YOU CAN TRY THIS...

– Sprinkle some fresh breadcrumbs over the timbale before cooking.

AUBERGINE LASAGNE

SERVES: 4 | **PREP:** 15 MINUTES | **COOK:** 2¾ HOURS

2 aubergines (eggplants), trimmed and sliced lengthways

3 tbsp olive oil, plus extra for brushing

2 onions, finely chopped

2 large carrots, diced

3 celery sticks, diced

2 garlic cloves, crushed

450g/1lb (2 cups) lean minced (ground) beef

240ml/8fl oz (1 cup) milk

300ml/10floz (1¼ cups) red wine

1 x 400g/14oz can (2 cups) chopped tomatoes

1 tbsp tomato purée (paste)

leaves stripped from a few sprigs of oregano or basil

12 lasagne sheets

3 tbsp grated Parmesan cheese

15g/½oz (1 tbsp) butter, diced

sea salt and freshly ground black pepper

You can make and assemble the lasagne in advance and leave it in a cool place for a few hours before the final baking in the oven. Note that the longer you cook the ragu (minced beef and vegetable sauce), the better it will taste.

1 Arrange the aubergine slices on a baking tray (cookie sheet) and brush lightly with oil. Cook under a preheated hot grill (broiler) for 3–4 minutes each side until tender and golden brown. Remove and cool.

2 Heat the olive oil in a large saucepan set over a medium heat and cook the onions, carrots, celery and garlic, stirring occasionally, for 8–10 minutes until softened but not browned. Stir in the beef and cook, stirring, for 4–5 minutes, until browned.

3 Add the milk and cook for a few minutes until most of it is absorbed by the meat and vegetables. Add the red wine, tomatoes, tomato purée and herbs. Reduce the heat and simmer gently for about 2 hours until you have a richly coloured, reduced mixture. Season to taste with salt and pepper.

4 Meanwhile, make the white sauce: melt the butter in a small pan over a low heat and stir in the flour to make a roux, stirring it to leave the sides of the pan clean. Cook for 1 minute then start whisking in the milk, a little at a time, until all of it has been added and there are no lumps. Increase the heat and stir with a wooden spoon until the sauce thickens and coats the back of the spoon. Season with nutmeg, salt and pepper.

For the white sauce:
60g/2oz (¼ cup) butter
60g/2oz (½ cup) plain
   (all-purpose) flour
480ml/16fl oz (2 cups) milk
a pinch of nutmeg

5 Preheat the oven to 200°C, 400°F, gas mark 6. Lightly oil or butter a large ovenproof dish.

6 Assemble the lasagne: arrange a layer of lasagne sheets in the bottom of the dish and spoon over half the beef ragu sauce. Cover with overlapping aubergine slices and another layer of lasagne. Pour a little of the white sauce over the lasagne and then add the remaining beef ragu and aubergine slices. Add another layer of lasagne and pour the rest of the white sauce over the top right to the edges of the dish. Sprinkle with Parmesan and dot with butter.

7 Bake in the preheated oven for about 20 minutes until bubbling, crisp and golden brown. Serve hot with some salad.

OR YOU CAN TRY THIS...
– Use minced (ground) pork or chicken instead of beef.
– Substitute white wine for the red.
– Fry or bake the aubergine slices instead of grilling (broiling) them.

PERSIAN STUFFED AUBERGINES

SERVES: 4 | **PREP:** 15 MINUTES | **COOK:** 1 HOUR

4 medium aubergines
(eggplants), trimmed
4 tbsp olive oil
2 large onions, chopped
3 garlic cloves, crushed
1 tsp cumin seeds
1 tsp ground cinnamon
1 tsp paprika
450g/1lb (2 cups) minced
(ground) lean lamb
3 tbsp pine nuts
2 tsp tomato purée (paste)
2 large tomatoes, diced
a pinch of sugar
a handful of flat-leaf parsley,
chopped
sea salt and freshly ground
black pepper
crusty bread and salad,
to serve

Stuffed aubergines make a simple supper dish or you can leave them to go cold and serve them for lunch the following day.

1 Preheat the oven to 190°C, 375°F, gas mark 5.

2 Cut the aubergines in half lengthways. Heat the oil in a large frying pan (skillet) set over a medium heat and cook the aubergine halves for 7–8 minutes each side until golden brown and softened. Remove from the pan and drain on kitchen paper (paper towels).

3 Add the onion and garlic to the pan and cook for 6–8 minutes until tender. Stir in the seeds and spices and cook for 1 minute. Add the lamb and pine nuts and cook, stirring, for 4–5 minutes until browned all over. Stir in the tomato purée, tomatoes and sugar and cook for 5 minutes. Add the parsley and season to taste.

4 Scoop a little of the flesh out of the aubergine halves and mix it into the lamb mixture. Use to fill the aubergine shells and place them in a large roasting tin (pan). Pour a little water into the tin around the aubergines and cook in the preheated oven for 20–25 minutes until cooked and golden brown.

5 Serve warm or cold with crusty bread and a crisp salad.

OR YOU CAN TRY THIS...
– Add some grated lemon zest, sultanas (seedless golden raisins)
  or a pinch of allspice to the lamb stuffing.
– You can fill red or green (bell) peppers and bake them in the same way.
– Use minced (ground) beef instead of lamb.
– Make a vegetarian version by omitting the meat and adding
  fresh breadcrumbs.

ROSEMARY ROAST CHICKEN WITH AUBERGINES

SERVES: 4 | **PREP:** 15 MINUTES | **COOK:** 1 HOUR 20 MINUTES

1 x 1.5kg/3lb whole chicken
1 large lemon
a few sprigs of rosemary
4 tbsp fruity olive oil,
    plus extra for drizzling
2 medium aubergines
    (eggplants), trimmed and
    cut into 2cm (¾in) thick
    rounds
leaves stripped from a few
    sprigs of thyme
240g/8oz (1 cup) natural
    yoghurt
a handful of dill, finely
    chopped
a handful of mint, finely
    chopped
pomegranate seeds, to garnish
sea salt and freshly ground
    black pepper
roast potatoes or couscous,
    to serve

Here's an easy and delicious lunch for a warm summer's weekend. It's great with salad, spinach or roasted vegetables.

1 Preheat the oven to 200°C, 400°F, gas mark 6.

2 Place the chicken in a large roasting tin (pan) and squeeze the juice out of the lemon over the top. Place the lemon halves inside the chicken cavity. Sprinkle with some leaves stripped from the rosemary sprigs and put the stems inside the chicken. Drizzle with a little olive oil and sprinkle with salt and pepper.

3 Arrange the aubergine rounds around the chicken and sprinkle the olive oil and thyme leaves over them.

4 Roast in the preheated oven for 1 hour 20 minutes until the chicken is cooked right through and the skin is crisp and appetisingly golden brown. Turn the aubergines over after 25 minutes to brown the other side. They may be cooked and tender well ahead of the chicken. If so, remove them from the pan and keep warm until the chicken is ready to carve and serve. You can test whether the chicken is cooked by inserting a thin skewer behind a leg – the juices should run clear.

5 Mix the yoghurt, dill and mint in a bowl and grind over a little black pepper. Scatter the pomegranate seeds over the top.

6 Let the chicken rest for a few minutes before carving. Serve with the aubergines and yoghurt with a bowl of roast potatoes or couscous.

OR YOU CAN TRY THIS...
– Use fresh oregano instead of thyme.
– Stir some pomegranate molasses or a dash of harissa into the yoghurt.
– Substitute tzatziki for the yoghurt.
– This works equally well with roast lamb.

MELANZANE ALLA PARMIGIANA

SERVES: 4 | **PREP:** 15 MINUTES | **SALT:** 30 MINUTES | **COOK:** 50 MINUTES–1 HOUR

1.3kg/3lb aubergines
    (eggplants), trimmed
sea salt, for sprinkling
flour, for dusting
olive oil, for frying
    and drizzling
300g/10oz mozzarella
    di bufala, thinly sliced
1 small bunch of basil, torn
100g/3½oz (1 cup)
    grated Parmesan
60g/2oz (1 cup) fresh
    white breadcrumbs
salad leaves, to serve

For the tomato sauce:
2 tbsp olive oil
3 garlic cloves, crushed
2 x 400g/14oz cans (4 cups)
    chopped tomatoes
120ml/4fl oz (½ cup) robust
    red wine
a pinch of sugar
sea salt and freshly ground
    black pepper

This baked aubergine dish is quintessentially Mediterranean, and different versions exist in southern Italy.

1 Cut the aubergines into thin slices lengthways. Put them in a colander and sprinkle with salt. Set aside for 30 minutes.

2 Meanwhile, make the tomato sauce: heat the oil in a saucepan set over a medium heat. Add the garlic and cook for 1–2 minutes without browning. Add the tomatoes and wine and bring to the boil. Reduce the heat and cook for 15–20 minutes until the sauce reduces and thickens. Season with sugar, salt and pepper.

3 Blitz the tomato sauce until smooth in a blender or food processor or purée with a hand-held electric blender.

4 Preheat the oven to 190°C, 375°F, gas mark 5. Rinse the salt off the aubergines under cold running water and pat dry with kitchen paper (paper towels). Dust with flour.

5 Shallow-fry the aubergines, in batches, in olive oil in a large frying pan (skillet) set over a high heat until golden brown on both sides. Remove with a slotted spoon and drain on kitchen paper.

6 Lightly oil a large ovenproof baking dish and put a layer of aubergine slices in the bottom. Pour some of the tomato sauce over the top and cover with mozzarella and some of the torn basil. Keep layering up the dish in this way, finishing with an aubergine layer. Sprinkle the Parmesan and breadcrumbs over the top and drizzle with olive oil.

7 Bake in the preheated oven for 25–30 minutes until crisp and golden brown. Serve warm, rather than hot, sprinkled with the remaining torn basil, and with a salad.

OR YOU CAN TRY THIS...
– If you're in a hurry, use passata instead of making the tomato sauce.
– Use fragrant fresh tomatoes when they're in season rather than canned.

AUBERGINE 'CANNELLONI'

SERVES: 4 | **PREP:** 20 MINUTES | **COOK:** 1 HOUR

2 large aubergines
(eggplants), trimmed
olive oil, for drizzling
400g/14oz spinach, tough
stalks removed
1 tbsp water
250g/9oz (generous 1 cup)
ricotta
1 tsp grated nutmeg
2 free-range egg yolks
85g/3oz (generous ¾ cup)
grated Parmesan
90ml/3fl oz (generous
¼ cup) crème fraîche
sea salt and freshly ground
black pepper
salad leaves, to serve

For the tomato sauce:
2 tbsp olive oil
1 onion, diced
3 garlic cloves, crushed
1 x 400g/14oz can (2 cups)
chopped tomatoes
1 tsp tomato purée (paste)
a pinch of sugar
a few drops of
balsamic vinegar

This is a skinny, healthy version of the traditional dish made with rolled-up sliced aubergine instead of pasta tubes. You can assemble the dish an hour or so in advance.

1 Preheat the oven to 200°C, 400°F, gas mark 6. Lightly oil 2 baking trays (cookie sheets).

2 Cut the aubergines into thin slices lengthways. Place them on the baking trays and drizzle with olive oil. Bake in the preheated oven for 15 minutes until tender and golden brown. Remove and leave to cool.

3 While the aubergines are cooking, make the tomato sauce. Heat the oil in a saucepan and cook the onion and garlic, stirring occasionally, over a medium heat for about 8 minutes until tender. Add the tomatoes and tomato purée and simmer gently for 10–15 minutes until reduced and thickened. Season to taste with the sugar, balsamic vinegar and some salt and pepper.

4 Make the filling: put the spinach in a heavy-based saucepan with the water. Cover with a lid and cook gently for 3–4 minutes until the leaves wilt and turn bright green. Drain in a colander, pressing down well with a small plate or saucer to squeeze out any excess juice.

5 Chop the spinach coarsely and mix with the ricotta, nutmeg, egg yolks and one-third of the Parmesan. Season lightly.

6 Spread the filling over the aubergine slices and roll up. Arrange them, seam-side down, in a shallow ovenproof baking dish. Pour the tomato sauce over the top and dot with the crème fraîche. Sprinkle with the remaining Parmesan.

7 Bake in the oven for about 20 minutes until golden brown. Serve hot with some salad

BAKING & PRESERVES

AUBERGINE CHOCOLATE CAKE

SERVES: 10 | **PREP:** 20 MINUTES | **COOK:** 1 HOUR

200g/7oz (scant 1 cup) unsalted butter, plus extra for greasing
450g/1lb aubergines (eggplants)
6 medium free-range eggs
200g/7oz (scant 1 cup) caster (superfine) sugar
225g/8oz dark (semisweet) chocolate (70% minimum cocoa solids)
85g/3oz (¾ cup) cocoa powder
150g/5oz (1 cup) ground almonds
icing (confectioner's) sugar or cocoa powder, for dusting

Adding aubergine to a cake may sound odd, but it makes it deliciously moist. You can serve this at teatime or for a dessert with some fresh fruit and crème fraîche or ice cream.

1 Preheat the oven to 180C, 350°F, gas mark 4. Grease a 23cm (9in) loose-bottomed (springform) cake tin (pan) and line with baking parchment (parchment paper).

2 Pierce the aubergines with a thin skewer and place on a plate. Cover with cling film (plastic wrap) and microwave on high for about 8 minutes or until softened. When they are cool enough to handle, scoop out the flesh and blitz it in a blender until smooth.

3 In a large bowl, beat the eggs and sugar with an electric whisk until really pale and fluffy.

4 Melt the butter and chocolate in a bowl suspended over a pan of just-simmering water. Remove from the heat as soon as they are melted.

5 With a large metal spoon, gently fold the butter and chocolate into the beaten eggs and sugar in a deep figure-of-eight movement, until the mixture is evenly coloured. Fold in the cocoa and ground almonds in the same way. Finally, fold in the aubergine. Take care not to over-mix.

6 Spoon the mixture into the prepared tin and bake in the preheated oven for about 45 minutes. You can test whether the cake is cooked by inserting a thin skewer into the centre. If it comes out clean, it's ready. If not, pop it back in the oven for a few more minutes.

7 After 15 minutes of cooling in the tin, turn the cake out onto a wire rack and leave to cool completely. Peel off the lining paper and dust the cake with icing sugar or cocoa before cutting into slices.

MELANZANE AL CIOCCOLATO

SERVES: 8 | **PREP:** 25 MINUTES | **COOK:** 15 MINUTES | **CHILL:** OVERNIGHT

2 large aubergines
(eggplants), trimmed
and peeled
flour, for dusting
6 tbsp olive oil
115g/4oz (½ cup) caster
(superfine) sugar
½ tsp ground cinnamon
grated zest of 1 large lemon
fresh strawberries or
raspberries, to serve

For the ricotta filling:
400g/14oz (scant 2 cups)
ricotta
2 medium free-range eggs,
beaten
60g/2oz (¼ cup) caster
(superfine) sugar
60g/2oz amaretti, crushed
60g/2oz (scant ½ cup)
blanched almonds,
chopped
30g/1oz candied orange
peel, diced

For the chocolate sauce:
240ml/8fl oz (1 cup) double
(heavy) cream
225g/8oz dark (semiweet)
chocolate (minimum 70%
cocoa solids)

This layered dessert from Naples and the Amalfi coast is traditionally eaten on Ferragosto (15 August) for the feast of the Assumption. It's a national holiday in Italy and the official start of the summer holiday season. Chocolate and aubergines might sound like a bizarre combination but they are surprisingly good.

1 Cut the aubergines lengthways into thin slices and dust lightly with flour. Heat the oil in a large frying pan (skillet) set over a medium heat and fry the aubergines in batches for 2–3 minutes each side until golden. Remove with a slotted spoon and drain on kitchen paper (paper towels).

2 Line a large plate or baking tray (cookie sheet) with kitchen paper and arrange the aubergines on it. Dredge them with the sugar, cinnamon and lemon zest.

3 Make the ricotta filling: mix the ricotta with the eggs and sugar until smooth and then stir in the remaining ingredients.

4 Make the chocolate sauce: heat the cream in a pan set over a low heat until it's hot and simmering. Remove from the heat. Break the chocolate into small pieces and stir gently into the cream until it melts and you have a smooth sauce. Set aside for the sauce to cool a little and thicken.

5 Assemble the dessert: lightly butter an ovenproof baking dish and line the bottom with overlapping aubergine slices. Cover with a layer of the ricotta mixture, drizzle with the chocolate sauce and then cover with another layer of aubergines. Continue layering up the dish in this way, finishing with a layer of aubergines and topping with chocolate sauce.

6 Chill in the fridge overnight until the chocolate sauce and ricotta layers set. Serve cold, cut into slices or squares, with a bowl of fresh strawberries or raspberries.

SPANISH BERENJENA PICKLE

MAKES: APPROX. 1KG/2LB 4OZ | **PREP:** 20 MINUTES | **COOK:** 15 MINUTES
PICKLE: 4–5 DAYS

2 large red (bell) peppers
1kg/2lb 4oz small baby
    aubergines (eggplants),
    with stems attached
6 garlic cloves,
    coarsely crushed
1 tbsp sweet paprika
    (pimentón)
1 tbsp cumin seeds
1 tsp fennel seeds
1 tbsp salt
360ml/12fl oz (1½ cups)
    red wine vinegar
120ml/4fl oz (½ cup)
    extra virgin olive oil

In Spain, whole baby aubergines are often pickled in oil and vinegar spiced with pimento. The authentic recipe uses tiny green Manchego aubergines, but you can use any purple, green or white baby ones. You can serve them with tapas or roasted chicken and meat.

1 Place the whole red peppers under a preheated hot grill (broiler) for a few minutes, turning them occasionally, until the skins are blistered and charred all over. Remove and set aside until they are cool enough to handle. Peel off the skins and remove the seeds and white ribs. Thinly slice the flesh.

2 Trim the ends of the stems on the aubergines, leaving the stems and calyxes intact. Bring the aubergines to the boil in a large pan of salted water and cook vigorously for 8–10 minutes until they are slightly tender but not mushy. Drain and rinse under cold running water in a colander. Pat dry with kitchen paper (paper towels).

3 Blitz the garlic, paprika, seeds, salt, vinegar and olive oil in a blender. Stir in the red pepper.

4 Put the drained aubergines in some sterilised glass jars (see page 104) and pour the flavoured oil and vinegar mixture over them. Add enough cold water to submerge the aubergines and nearly fill the jars.

5 Screw the lids tightly onto the jars and leave in a cool, dry place for 4–5 days before consuming. Once opened, store them in the fridge.

OR YOU CAN TRY THIS...

– Use cider, white wine or sherry vinegar instead of red wine vinegar.
– Substitute yellow or green (bell) peppers for the red ones.
– Add some ground cinnamon or ginger.
– Try adding a little honey, like the Spanish sometimes do.

INDIAN-SPICED BRINJAL PICKLE

MAKES: APPROX. 1.5KG/3LB | **PREP:** 15 MINUTES | **COOK:** 1 HOUR

4 tbsp sunflower oil

3 onions, diced

4 garlic cloves, crushed

85g/3oz fresh root ginger, peeled and diced

2 red chillies, deseeded and diced

1 tbsp black mustard seeds

2 tsp coriander seeds, crushed

8 curry leaves

1 tsp ground cumin

3 tbsp tamarind paste

3 tbsp tomato purée (paste)

175g/6oz (generous 1 cup) sultanas (seedless golden raisins)

1kg/2lb 4oz aubergines (eggplants), trimmed and cubed

200g/7oz (scant 1 cup) soft light brown sugar

300ml/10floz (1¼ cups) malt vinegar

1 tsp salt

This hot aubergine pickle goes really well with curries, bhajis and samosas. Like other pickles and chutneys, it's best eaten several weeks after making.

1 Heat the oil in a large saucepan set over a low heat. Cook the onions, garlic and ginger, stirring occasionally, for 10–12 minutes until softened.

2 Stir in the chillies, seeds, curry leaves and cumin and cook for 2–3 minutes. Add the tamarind paste and tomato purée and cook for 2 minutes.

3 Stir in the sultanas, aubergines, sugar, vinegar and salt. Stir well until the sugar dissolves and then let the mixture simmer away gently for 30–40 minutes until the mixture thickens.

4 Meanwhile, sterilise some jars by popping some clean ones (lids off) into a very low oven at 110°C, 225°F, gas mark ¼ for about 20 minutes, then turn the oven off and leave the jars until you're ready to fill them.

5 Ladle the hot pickle into the sterilised jars and half-screw on the lids. When they are cool, tighten the lids, label the jars and store in a cool dark place. The chutney will keep unopened for several months. After opening, store in the fridge.

OR YOU CAN TRY THIS...

– Add some fenugreek or yellow mustard seeds.

– For a milder spicy pickle, leave out the chillies.

– Use cider, red wine or white wine vinegar instead of malt.

SEEDY AUBERGINE & TOMATO CHUTNEY

MAKES: APPROX. 1.5KG/3LB | **PREP:** 15 MINUTES | **COOK:** 1¼–2 HOURS

1 tsp fenugreek seeds
6 tbsp sunflower oil
1 tbsp cumin seeds
2 tbsp black mustard seeds
2 large onions, chopped
2.5cm/1in piece fresh root
    ginger, peeled and diced
3 garlic cloves, crushed
1 red chilli, diced
1.5kg/3lb tomatoes,
    skinned and chopped
2 medium aubergines
    (eggplants), trimmed
    and cubed
450g/1lb (2 cups) sugar
300ml/½ pint (1¼ cups)
    malt vinegar
1 tsp sea salt

You can eat this chutney straight away but it will taste even better if you leave it in the kitchen cupboard for two or three weeks so the flavours can deepen. It's a great accompaniment to curries, grilled (broiled) chicken and pork, or just some simple cheese and crackers.

1 Toast the fenugreek seeds in a dry frying pan (skillet) over a medium heat for 1–2 minutes, stirring occasionally. Remove from the pan and set aside to cool for a few minutes.

2 Heat the oil in a large heavy-based saucepan and cook the cumin, mustard and toasted fenugreek seeds over a low heat for 2–3 minutes. Stir in the onions, ginger, garlic and chilli and cook gently for 10 minutes until softened.

3 Add the tomatoes, aubergines and sugar and simmer gently for 15 minutes, stirring occasionally to dissolve the sugar. Stir in the vinegar and salt and simmer gently until the mixture thickens to a syrupy chutney-like consistency without any liquid. Be patient – this might take anything from 40 minutes up to 1¼ hours. Stir the chutney regularly to prevent it catching and burning on the bottom of the pan.

4 Meanwhile, sterilise some jars by popping some clean ones (lids off) into a very low oven at 110°C, 225°F, gas mark ¼ for about 20 minutes, then turn the oven off and leave the jars until you're ready to fill them.

5 Ladle the hot chutney into the sterilised jars and half-screw on the lids. When they are cool, tighten the lids, label the jars and store in a cool, dark place. The chutney will keep unopened for several months. After opening, store in the fridge.

OR YOU CAN TRY THIS...
– Add some sultanas (seedless golden raisins).
– Add some cubed pumpkin or apples for sweetness.
– Use red or white wine vinegar instead of malt.

ITALIAN PICKLED AUBERGINES

MAKES: APPROX. 1KG/2LB 4OZ | **PREP:** 20 MINUTES | **SALT:** 1 HOUR
DRAIN: 12 HOURS | **COOK:** 2–3 MINUTES | **PICKLE:** 2 WEEKS

900g/2lb aubergines
   (eggplants), trimmed
1 tsp salt
240ml/8fl oz (1 cup) water
240ml/8fl oz (1 cup) white
   wine vinegar
1 red (bell) pepper,
   deseeded and
   finely chopped
2 red chillies, deseeded
   and shredded
6 garlic cloves, peeled
   and halved
2 tsp dried oregano
a handful of flat-leaf parsley,
   chopped
480ml/16fl oz (2 cups)
   extra virgin olive oil

In southern Italy, where it's served either as part of the antipasto or with grilled (broiled) and roasted meat, cold cuts, cheese and olives or just country bread, this pickle is known as *melanzane sott'olio* (if oil is added, as below) or *sotto aceto* (if pickled in vinegar).

1 Thinly slice the aubergines lengthways and then cut each slice into long strips. Place them in a colander and sprinkle with the salt. Weight them down with a plate topped with a weight or a heavy can. Leave for at least 1 hour to exude any excess liquid.

2 Gently press down on the aubergines and squeeze out any remaining liquid. Put them in a large saucepan with the water and vinegar and bring to the boil. Allow to boil for 2–3 minutes maximum (no more or the aubergines will lose their crispness and go soggy). Drain the aubergines in a colander.

3 Cover and set aside to drain for at least 12 hours. Gently pat the aubergine dry with kitchen paper (paper towels). Mix the aubergine strips with the red pepper, chillies, garlic and dried and chopped herbs.

4 Meanwhile, sterilise some glass jars by popping some clean ones (lids off) into a very low oven at 110°C, 225°F, gas mark ¼ for about 20 minutes, then turn the oven off and leave the jars until cool.

5 Divide the aubergine mixture among the jars and slowly pour the olive oil over them until everything is completely submerged. Screw on the lids tightly, label the jars and store in a cool, dark place for at least 2 weeks before consuming. The pickle will keep well unopened for 3 months. After opening, store in the fridge.

OR YOU CAN TRY THIS...
– Use a green (bell) pepper and chillies instead of red.
– Try chopped basil or mint, or add some sprigs of thyme or rosemary.

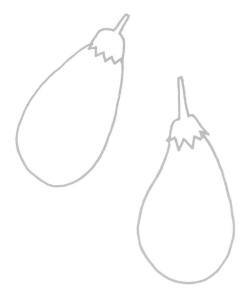

10 9 8 7 6 5 4 3 2 1

Ebury Press, an imprint of Ebury Publishing,
20 Vauxhall Bridge Road,
London SW1V 2SA

Ebury Press is part of the Penguin Random House group of companies
whose addresses can be found at global.penguinrandomhouse.com

Design: Louise Evans
Photography: Joff Lee
Food stylist: Mari Williams
Editor: Jessica Barnfield

First published by Ebury Press in 2018

www.eburypublishing.co.uk

A CIP catalogue record for this book is available from the British Library

ISBN 9781785038877

Printed and bound in China by Toppan Leefung

Penguin Random House is committed to a sustainable future for our
business, our readers and our planet. This book is made from Forest
Stewardship Council® certified paper.